Sailing through Life

My Life with God, Spirituality, and Sexuality

Elvira Divina Fernandes

BALBOA
PRESS

A DIVISION OF HAY HOUSE

Andrew Asthon Stafford: (cover), and picture 592
A. Wilson pictures: 1900 - 3417
Francisca Lopes: picture 2361

Balboa Press books may be ordered through booksellers or by contacting:

Balboa Press
A Division of Hay House
1663 Liberty Drive
Bloomington, IN 47403
www.balboapress.com.au
1 (877) 407-4847

Because of the dynamic nature of the Internet, any web addresses or links contained in this book may have changed since publication and may no longer be valid. The views expressed in this work are solely those of the author and do not necessarily reflect the views of the publisher, and the publisher hereby disclaims any responsibility for them.

The author of this book does not dispense medical advice or prescribe the use of any technique as a form of treatment for physical, emotional, or medical problems without the advice of a physician, either directly or indirectly. The intent of the author is only to offer information of a general nature to help you in your quest for emotional and spiritual well-being. In the event you use any of the information in this book for yourself, which is your constitutional right, the author and the publisher assume no responsibility for your actions.

Any people depicted in stock imagery provided by Thinkstock are models, and such images are being used for illustrative purposes only. Certain stock imagery © Thinkstock.

Printed in the United States of America.

ISBN: 978-1-4525-1406-2 (sc)
ISBN: 978-1-4525-1405-5 (e)

Balboa Press rev. date: 05/09/2014

To all readers: my intention is to share my life experience in a way that inspires you to live in courage, faith, joy, and realisation of your dreams at any point in your lifetime. Consider yourself always an eternal being of light, which you are free to turn on.

Contents

Acknowledgements

I thank and honour my parents—to my father's memories and soul, and to my mother, for being my channel to this planet in my physical world.

I thank and honour the beautiful being and soul of my son, Diego, for being my lighthouse with his unconditional love and non-judgement, bringing me to the shore in my journey's safety.

I thank and honour everyone who came across my life's journey and contributed in one way or another, making me a better person and making this project possible.

I thank and honour my brothers and sisters, all my relatives, teachers, authors, and friends for their support and loving messages throughout my life.

I thank and honour my spiritual guides, my own light, which makes all things possible for me as my wish.

Forgiving others and ourselves is nothing, but a kind of gesture to let go of a rotten imagination that no longer serves us.

—Elvira Divina Fernandes

Introduction

This book started by approaching how to walk in this lifetime on Earth, living with sexuality and God. I always had the intention of passing the message of the sacred side of a reunion of man and woman in the physical perspective without leaving the divinity outside of one life's context. I had no preconceptions regarding religious beliefs, shame, guilt, and fear of expressing oneself. It is intrinsic in any passage of years that I was always seeking a balance between those two things, regardless of where I was.

I know that many people think as I do, but how many would either question or bring it up? It became big, living in the first phase of my life in a completely different society where I lived after my thirties. However, in essence, I always had to understand and feel those two senses of living, from a country in development to a first-world country's mentality. There would not be differences, as it comes from our inner beings, but culture counts. My biggest challenge was the language. I still remember when I sat on the curb at twilight in a suburb of Sydney, completely lost, without knowing how to communicate. The street was deserted. I was coming from the nearest shopping centre, which was about five kilometres away from home. I got off the bus in the middle of my way back; it was a weekend, when the bus schedule runs different from the weekdays. I didn't know anything about all those basic needs and was truly lost, with no chance to get one step ahead. For the first time in my life, in my thirties, I understood the reason for babies and kids crying; I felt it under my skin. I could not talk, even if I had someone around to talk to. I was lonely, lost, and hopeless; after a long wait, which for me felt like eternity, a free taxi came and stopped when I signalled. It took me back home with my shopping bags and my next painful foreign experience.

But language would not be my biggest challenge, as I had overcome that barrier sooner than I thought by going to school and improving my language skills. There are two things that will be brought up again and again every single time we breathe as human beings. (Maybe in one lifetime or more—who knows!) There is not enough time to learn about them, as they are part of the human race's evolution, and they will be part of us here, now, and forever, beyond death. They may be the only two tools that move us to grow in the physical and spiritual perspectives at the same time. I stop and ask myself: "In the adult population walking on this planet, how many have thought at least once about God and sex?"

So, when reading my life story, you will be thinking about those two aspects, more than once, either understanding or not, asking questions. Perhaps you will have no immediate answers, because we all need to find our own, not being swayed by others' opinions or our own inner wisdom for the exact moment we are standing in our eternity line in this lifetime.

Each moment and each action we go through, we are guided through our physical and spiritual world. It makes our lives interesting, and our biggest task is to live in balance, finding peace in our hearts. As I heard from one of my good teachers in life, Peggy Phoenix Dubro: "Think with your heart, and feel with your mind."

I'm curious: What if human beings had the same intelligence, only what are called good principles in life, and had neither religion's nor any philosophy's guidance—how would it be taken? What would be the concepts of "God," and how would "sexuality" impact our lives?

Chapter One

One More New Beginning

I looked older than my age, taller than average girls of my age, and very different, as I had fair skin and blue eyes. Wherever I went, I would be seen as different physically; I was very eye-catching for boys, mostly for those a bit older than me. One of my sisters loved to take me with her to social events and parties and always made sure I was spotlessly dressed up and looking perfect and on fashion. At thirteen, I had my first boyfriend, who was introduced to me by my sister and her friend, my brother's girlfriend. He was the most gorgeous guy in town and wanted by all the girls his age and younger. But I couldn't wait to get home and hide myself from that guy.

It was like being induced to go out and to have a boyfriend. Being so young, I was not able to make up my mind, so for some reason, I was going with the flow and peers' influences. That was not making me feel happy. It happened in a different part of my own town, and I couldn't wait to get home. Then I could avoid it all by not going out.

All the guys from the neighbouring towns used to turn up, and there was Len, after me like a hunter over his prey. I was feeling safe inside my parents' carriage, wrapped in a blanket. I made sure I had my head covered and no one could see me leaving town in the dark, heading to our country house for the weekend with my parents. I was not yet prepared to understand and enjoy flirting, but I knew that connecting with nature used to put me in my best state of being, even without understanding and expressing any feeling.

Human beings can call their attention on God's concept and existence and the myths created about sex, regardless of the religious beliefs we were brought up with.

We can create arts, such as music, painting, poetry, and so on. In doing so, we are getting closer to God. We still can cultivate our physical world, starting with our bodies, giving to it the ultimate physical intimacy's energy. This can make us vibrate high and with love, and love is God!

For me, having sex at this age would be the last thing I would know about, and more than that, the first thing to be prohibited. It was there inside me, sleeping deeply instead of waking up to life, as was God.

I was born in a rural area, in a town of three thousand people and attended up to middle school in a little farm. I come from a family of six brothers and three sisters. From year one at school, I used to walk at least three kilometres with three of my brothers and some other kids from our neighbourhood to reach the school. Then we had to move to town to attend high school.

I had a great childhood, living in true communion with nature. I was surrounded by domestic animals and wildlife, beautiful flora, an abundance of organic food, rivers and streams of crystalline water in which to play and swim. My parents were very strict in raising us, mostly my mother, as she had a very strong personality. A hard worker and very spiritual also, she used to help everyone in the neighbourhood in healing their children, just setting her hands on them in prayer. She became popular by doing so, until my father decided to move to town, to take me to the next grade at school.

Neither of my parents attended school beyond primary grades, but they wanted us to keep going and get more education than they had. This was a very common thought in our society at this point in time.

I am the youngest in the family, and ever since I was very little, I've loved reading. But we were only allowed to read the old book of our church or the school's language book and do homework on a daily basis after finishing our home duties. Everyone was supposed to help at the farm and with housekeeping from a very early age. The boys were supposed to help with "men's" duties, and the girls were supposed to do "women's" duties, such as cleaning, laundry, cooking, and sewing. This was also a very common thought in our society at this time.

I had moved many times in my life. I will come back later to my teenage years, but now I will try to give more information regarding what this book is about.

It is said that we never learn enough until we die, and I always had very deep within me the craving to learn more and more about everything I could. I was always going forward, regardless of whether I knew very much about what I was doing; that was why I was sometimes called adventurous or even crazy. I always considered myself a lucky person, and more than mental, a spiritual person. At the same time, I always kept a strong, energetic physical body. So my life experiences and tributes instilled in me the understanding and meaning of the two things that every one of us would question one day in life and that could happen at any point in our lifetime. And nothing better represents spirituality as God and the physical as sex. We get caught by the complexity of our biological body and our spiritual world inside the context of our beings, values, or inside the context of those beliefs that we were brought up with.

I believe there is not such a concept that we can define in a way anyone can read; it is all about what each one of us feels and believes. However, anyone can perceive that everyone's behaviour will carry it on intrinsically, in disguise.

I know that I was smashed on both sides: my spirituality as well as my sexuality. But that all makes sense when we go back in time and review our society's values and our religious values' influence. In essence, we all have free will to choose where to go and to take the path that will give us the life experience we need to find our own answers and be the person we want to be—or simply be who we really are and coexist in humankind with our spiritual being as one.

Time went on, and flirts were coming and going—more for fun than for any other things. So it is with all peers until teenagers fall in love for the first time.

I had the experience of falling in love for the first time with a guy who didn't fall for me; it seemed to be just for suffering and remembering. That was spiritual: love. That was a kind of God inside, sleeping, waiting to be ignited by my physical body, but nothing was happening.

The rule was: girls cannot have sex with any other man, only with her husband, and they're supposed to get married while they're still a virgin. Otherwise it would be a reason for discrimination by the church and by society.

I did know well about the "thing called sexuality." No one ever told me about it; I just felt things happening with my body. Sometimes when I was riding my horse or a push bike and my genitals were pressed against it, I used to have good feelings that took me to the stars. There was no sexual education at school, because it was forbidden. I remember at school once, I was asked to leave and go back home because I was wearing a pair of long pants that were skin-coloured, loose and thick, with no transparency. We were allowed to wear any clothing, as the school had no rules for uniforms. I really never understood what was wrong with those pants, as I would say they were more serious and discreet than any of the other girls'.

Until this point, I just knew that I used to get goose bumps and feel burning inside when some boyfriend would kiss me in a flash. I was always running away, and I surely would not answer if you asked me what boys' and girls' friends used to do. Maybe dance together, hold hands, walk and sit in the park, talk, go to the cinema; not more than that.

I was up to the time of my first big challenge and disappointment. One of my schoolmates— someone I only had interest in as a good friend—brought me to my first big, painful move. It all started when someone came and told my sister and me that he was saying in town that he had received an anonymous letter from a girl. He suspected the letters were coming from me, and he was saying that the author of the letter feared that she was pregnant.

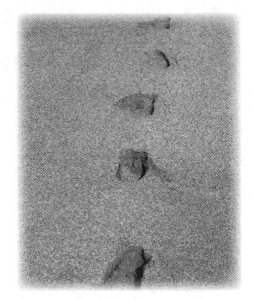

How could a Catholic virgin be under such an unfair accusation that would drag any girl's reputation through the mud? That fell like a bomb on my head and my life, mostly because I was passive and would never have the capability to stand up to defend myself. I would never have any idea where to start from; I felt myself in such an embarrassing position.

I still didn't have too much to do but let things go, and the truth would come up—later. The result was that I didn't speak with him afterwards for five years. I'm sure we missed a great friendship for all this time.

Like many teenagers, I also fell for my maths teacher and another heartbreak after the breakup by parents and things once more with pain and disappointment.

As I said, there were always the church duties to carry on and follow, in parallel with school and life development, under the eyes of a small community. Everyone knows, talks, and participates in others' business. Honestly, that was one thing I just used to accept; no matter that I had nothing to hide according to the law, church, and a good family's reputation. That wasn't a place for me, and that I was definitely sure about. So with the church, there was one important thing always on my heart and my mind: despite being a follower and never rebelling against any of those laws, I always felt there was something else to be known. I just didn't know what was it, but I knew that one day, I would have it clear in my mind and mostly on my heart. I always believe we are born missing something big, and we will die seeking it. But we learn so much if we want to. There will always be a light for each one of us, regardless of beliefs, creeds, rules, or habits; we only need to turn that light on.

Those religious teachers could not make up my mind about love, forgiveness, compassion, or any other positive attitude and non-judgemental conduct, easily and forever. Of course, they intended to, with the same ability to make me keep in mind what was a sin and everything that would upset God and bring over me whatever would be punishment. I assure you that if I felt punished in my life, it was not by any kind of "God." But we are punished by humanity, its laws, and consequently society and its rules. And what is interesting: the teaching starts at an early age, when we are all vulnerable and unable to take the decision by speaking and standing up for ourselves. So, as children, we were already taking on the challenge of been modelled minds. It was easy as fresh-brained kids to assimilate and follow. That would not be hard, as we had the same roles at home as our parents; we were already brainwashed to do the same and continue the chain.

However, from the depths of my heart, I always had feelings that out there somewhere, it would be more than I had been told. I could always feel it, no matter that I had never the words to express it. Those feelings were there, more alive than ever. They were oppressed under all those times of closure that I lived, until the point in my life when I started seeking my one answer on my way. I also thought that was "out there" and kept seeking.

I had read some Buddhist concepts that say we get to the point where we come from nowhere, going to "nowhere". These concepts would make some sense to me at some point in my life. They helped me to understand that there were other teachings for us, beyond only those we were brought up with. So you can see clearly that these were not teaching you anything, only giving you more doubt to be cleared ahead in life. That was challenging and positive for my view.

I take from the point that we are born as a being of clear light; all the teachings that are poured onto us will be like the clouds covering the shining of our original light, until we are able to blow that cloud away and shine it back. That light, for me, is God. I would go a bit further and say: *there is no gender on light.* So who are we supposed to obey? I could call the answer: this is God, but this is us too. And all this is also simple. Talking about gender, I found that the most conflicting and painful issue for a woman in my generation was the way to deal with sensuality in the middle of so many oppressive religious roles designed to shape women's behaviours.

We are in the third millennium AD, and still some husbands still assert total control over their wives, even after they have separated, using "Gods' Forgiveness" as a weapon.

I grew up under beliefs that God was an old, bearded man, ready to punish everyone who disobeyed his rules. For some reason, those rules would always be favourable to males. I started mentioning that the concept of *obeying* was created for women only. The majority of time such as at home, in a marriage; at the office, where only men would be the boss; running countries on the top of roles in government houses in some different societies. I would say that it was not more than forty years ago.

This was just the beginning of my first big journey as a teenager, as I was leaving a town of three thousand people and moving to the capital, with a population of about fifteen million. One of my brothers and one of my sisters was living in the capital of our state long enough to have the experience to help me to take off on my own life, working and studying. I was leaving behind my parents, my brothers, my other sister, my nephews and nieces, and all the friends from my childhood, up to my high-school mates. That was a big change, and I just felt that

I should move, regardless of the feelings of sadness following me that made me cry all night during my five-hour coach trip.

At this point, I was eighteen years old. I had been visiting the capital with some relatives who had taken me to the beach when I was twelve years old. From that time on, I would never stop dreaming of being close to the ocean again. The sensation of swimming in salt water, playing with the waves, and walking in the sand would never leave me anymore. The capital was not too far from the nearest beach, and there would always be a chance to escape and be in heaven, as it was for me.

My first week in that concrete jungle, a lot started to happen. I lost myself and fell to tears, taking about two hours to get where I was supposed to be in thirty minutes. I could not stop crying at home, remembering the sadness of my sister left behind. Even before adapting myself, I was given a job at the same insurance company where my cousin used to work. I took a job as a clerk, regardless of my brother's insistence on keeping me focussed on my studies. He said that he would cover my expenses and keep me only studying. However, the craving for independence was there, and nothing could be done about it, as I determined to commit with both, working and studies. That was what I started to do. I would see nothing but joy, adventure, and a new life ahead, even though I could never define specifically what was about to happen next.

My cousin and I used to leave home early in the morning with lunch in our bags and take the bus to the office together. We became very close. After high school, I had started to do a bridge course to the university, every evening after work, up to eleven o'clock. She just loved to enjoy her spare time flirting around. She also was blonde, with big blue eyes, long hair, and skin as smooth as a porcelain doll. She would have any man she wanted in the blink of her eyes, from the office to out there socialising. She was always trying to bring me to her circle of friends and potential boyfriends, which was fun for my spare time. She chose living a bit more life and working, going to the Uni at her mature age, becoming a housewife and a solicitor.

A few weeks later, I started school and my life became busy, with no time for church anymore. The weekends were also filled with classes, intensive studies for the next big test for Uni. I dreamed at this point of becoming a veterinary doctor, which would cost me a lot of time. So I spent my minimal spare time with peers from school; it was practical and joyful too. We shared the same interests, and that was great.

After one year, I could not achieve enough points to pass in the first option of my career at the Uni. As working-class individuals, we could not give up on working for our own survival, as I said before, so I had to follow another career option. We didn't have help, like in a first-world country, no career advisors or abilities tests to help us find our best path in our intellectual development.

I had great time fulfilled with the purity of thoughts and behaviour with peers. Then a time came in my life that brought nothing but harassment from everywhere in my workplace. I will have to come back to this time later on, as it describes some of those big challenges related to the message of this work—walking on this planet with humankind caring on for God and sexuality!

Just because I have been an unusual person and even been called weird by many, it doesn't make me feel bad at all. I have to recognise that it is not very common for women my age to live life in a similar way to what I do. In my fifties, when I had to restart my life after being married for eighteen years, I took on what I thought was the greatest journey of my life. At the beginning of the year, I started a sailing trip from the east coast, across the top of Australia, towards western Australia, on board a thirty-eight-foot catamaran yacht. It started in Brisbane, the capital of Queensland, and went around the main islands and the Great Barrier Reef, across of the Gulf of Carpentaria, a journey of around five thousand nautical miles, before reaching the Cambridge Gulf, three hundred nautical miles before the Kimberley Coast. We would be cruising and stopping at the main cities' ports for supplies. Most of the trajectory was around inhabited islands and coastline, making the journey challenging.

About nine months earlier, I had met a man who became a good friend during the time I was recovering from my marital breakup. He was seeking someone to help him on his personal dream journey of sailing a bigger yacht than the one he had before, from the east coast to western Australia. He had also put some efforts into building a long-lasting relationship. I had something different planned for my new year ahead, which was easier to put on hold for a great sailing adventure. We spent a week after New Year's meeting our interests and clarifying conditions and plans, to see if we would be able to go ahead and give ourselves a chance to accomplish 100 per cent of our goals.

I believe in my determination and capability to deal with any circumstances; more than ever, I trust my intuition, and I knew that it would be a hard, complex journey. However, the outcome for me would not bring anything that wouldn't be positively accountable. Nothing was done without the freedom of choice to stop anytime for any reason that would not meet our satisfaction or discomfort. The deal was sealed, and to me, I have no other way but to focus on the experience and commitment of accomplishing the journey with responsibility, safety, and perfect communion with Mother Nature.

The beginning involved driving from the southwest coast up to the northern coast (around four thousand kilometres) during the wet season, and continuing on to the east coast, completing another six thousands kilometres, up to the beginning of the dry season (March). We purchased a sailboat and set it up for the sailing trip back in seven months, until the new wet season would start again. At the time, I had been working for about four years as a caregiver for people with special needs in my community.

My co-workers were constantly asking me, aren't you scared? Have you ever sailed before? I use to answer "no and no" for both questions, and that was true—no fear and never sailed before. I would add, "We could not fear the unknown." When I faced the challenges, I'd say how I felt. That was my statement, and honestly, that was the truth for me, so there I went.

There were detailed arrangements for the practical actions to be taken, plans for achieving the safest way of doing things, and some research about basic information on sailing. It was just the basics, as time was running out and there was not much time left for that, some training on safety, and dreams. The hopes and goals were to anchor the yacht in the Cambridge Gulf before the wet season started in November. The excitement could not be hidden from miles away, and I had the feeling of being back in my twenties again. The challenge was to help anchor the yacht at the ending point, as mentioned before. It was also the captain's first experience on that kind of yacht—which at least was better and more reliable than his first experience sailing a smaller yacht on a journey thousands of nautical miles less than two years earlier, with seven different people helping him as a crew along the way.

The journey started one hot and sunny day in the middle of February, after I settled my son to live with friends, at school, with his driver's licence and taking his own journey. That was my first lesson already; the feeling of leaving my son was more frightening than any other thing I would face out there on my own. But we both knew it would happen in one way or another for our own growth; my son and I were aware of it, and we just had to face it.

February 15: First thing in the morning, I finished packing, paid the last bills, and gave one big hug to my son. Now he was on his own legs. I have to confess, that was hard for both of us, but we had the best to hook on: the love we feel for each other and the natural commitment to support each other when needed. I wished to leave him a big written message, but I felt that would make things harder on him, so I decided not make the departure dramatic. I had learnt that drama is supposed to be in the back seat when we are driving our lives forward; that makes things easier.

The journey had really started. We had a long way to go by road yet; it is about seven thousand miles by land up to the east coast of Australia, where we planned to commence the sailing trip back to western Australia.

The past was left behind, and I was walking away from it, towards a new journey. I still had wounds in my heart to be healed, after my latest few years of therapy and spiritual self-development. Again I was in a "fool condition," according to One writing by Osho: (Osho Zen Tarot - The Transcendental Game of Zen"

> "Be a fool in the Taoist sense, in the Zen sense. Don't try to create a wall of knowledge around you. Whatsoever experience comes to you let it happen, and then go on dropping it. Go on cleaning your mind continuously; go on dying to the past so you remain in the present, here-now, as if just born, just as a baby. In the beginning it's going to be very difficult. The world will start to take advantage of you ... let them. They are poor fellows. Even if you are cheated, deceived and robbed, let it happen, because that which is really yours nobody can steal from you. And each time you don't allow situations to corrupt you that opportunity will become integration inside. Your soul will become more crystallized."

Those words remind me of the trust I always had in those around me; more than that, my good faith always helped me to trust straight away, with no judgment. Many of the times when I was deceived, I had a feeling of being foolish; however, I never felt anything was missing afterwards. Today, I feel that I am a fool every morning, and I ponder what I had learnt at the end of each day, without feeling that I have all that is supposed to be mine inside me. I am more convinced that it really cannot be taken away; it is uncorrupted. That thinking helped me to build up inside me the strength and the knowledge that the target really doesn't matter; what always matters is the source.

There was another short life to be lived before sunset. After a half day of driving, we arrived in Geraldton, did light shopping for supplies, and then set up for the night at the caravan park. This time, I was a few metres from the ocean, where I could have a nice swim and enjoy the afternoon before tea. There was not much time to enjoy, and we were caught by a sandstorm, burning my eyes and filling the tent with sand and strong wind blowing everything around.

It was the same sensation I'd felt in my past, where you have clear sight, and from time to time, like the storm, events take over and disturb your view. Back in my twenties, I was into my new experience of life, thirsty to start at the university and a new career. In my hometown, country people from the lower and middle class had no option only to study. They have to work to pay their own expenses and studies, so that means full-time work plus full-time studies. They start their work journeys in the early morning, ending at five in the afternoon, and start their studies around seven thirty in the evening, finishing up by eleven thirty. They have thirty days of holidays from work once a year and school holidays only in July and January. Some work the reverse way, working in the evenings and going to school during the daytime, particularly those who live in big cities with chances of working on night shifts.

I started to work in an office during the day; there was a good chance to start a nice career as a secretary. I was a very organized person, a hard worker, punctual, enthusiastic, with good manners and had some experience from my town.

After three months as a clerk, I was asked to cover for the secretaries on their days off and holidays. I thought that was a clear view of my personal résumé! I never realized that I was in the jungle, with lots of hunters looking for "new prey"; any innocent dream would be thrown away, and it would be hard to survive. The little bosses had their try to win, but they had their careers to look after, so they would go slowly with the harassment. They could jeopardise their position, so their fear was in my favour, and I'd win at this point.

In another month, I was covering the executive secretaries, from the top board of the company, so there was no fear of harassment. It was just a game of competition between them, except one of them who would go for my opposite gender. I remember that there was an unforgettable gesture of kindness: the company had its only bank, and we used to have our payroll with it. Every time I walked in to do my banking, a gentleman would stand up very promptly to serve me, breathlessly saying, "How is my Kim Novak today?"

I even didn't know who he was talking about. It made me blush when he kindly explained to me, "She is my preferred Hollywood star, and you remind me of her with your long, blonde, curled hair; with your white skin and red lipstick. You shake my heart when walking in on your high heels, making each step too long to get closer."

That is a sweet memory, such a breeze compared with the storm of harassment which would keep going on further and further from one job to another. I was even dismissed for trying over and over to overcome that challenge. Being harassed in my country hometown in the seventies was a huge issue for us women, as we did not have any kind of law to protect us. Each woman working as a secretary was subject to harassment and had developed the ability to keep principles, a job, and a good state of mind. Later on, I would realize how protected I was from something invisible to me at that time.

At the same time I was attacked, with not much effort from my side, as a woman who surely would not know how to defend herself with her own skills; a woman with no intention to play games or hurt others, but only pursuing a dream. There was certainly an invisible protection that I could call God! I cannot say that I would be happy finding a lover or companion, but that was a real disturbance before my eyes, like a sandstorm. I dreamed for a few seconds, as I did thirty years ago, and my inner being was advertising for sharing:

Needed:
Someone to share accommodation,
In a full sense.
Needed: someone who loves life,
Who smiles, who plays, goes, and comes back
With its eyes, ears and heart.
It is very important to be present in the mornings,
To pull up the zipper on my back,
To turn me around, checking my hair.

> Needed urgently: someone
> To lift me up on my heels and kiss me in the air.
> Someone to enlighten my room when I feel in shade.
> Needed: someone
> Simply to share.

As with any storm, it passed, and we had to keep going. We got back on the road. The wet season had started, and we heard on the news that the highway was closed due to flooding. The rain was quiet heavy in that area, and it would be possible to drive up in about three days, so we had to find a place to wait. The waiting time was supposed to be pleasant. We were in a city called Carnarvon, and about thirty-five kilometres towards to the coast, Will knew a place called blow hole, with good spots to get fresh food, such as oysters and delicious reef fish. That afternoon, we camped in the blow hole; it was very hot, and the sky was heavily loaded for the next rain.

In a couple of minutes, we had a line thrown in the water, with the intent of catching a fish for dinner. The water was crystalline, and we could see every grain of sand at the bottom and in between the rocks. Suddenly I saw a school of fish; I could not describe their beauty. It was a mix of purple, pink, green, and blue stripes, and they were many of different sizes, swinging with the waves in such magnificent movements! I was stunned and submerged with them in that ballet, when suddenly my line was pulled and I felt that I had hooked one. I kept pulling it up to the top of the reef, and there was a beautiful, two-kilo fish. I felt tears, and the last thing I would do was kill and eat such a nice fish.

Ali jumped, and I said, "I'll put that fish back; we will eat an ugly one."

He replied, "There won't be an ugly fish around here. They all are fishes to be eaten."

Then I said, "So we won't have fresh dinner!"

The idea to eat the fish wasn't bad if I had not gone with them in the moment when they were providing me the most beautiful spectacle I had even seen. In the water, their beautiful colours and synchronised movements made me travel to heaven for minutes and provided me healing with that view. There was no disagreement about the decision to eat only the ugly fish from that day on, but honouring each one of them in the same proportion for our grateful food supply.

A few minutes later, Will caught another fish, and before I could see it closer, he had it ready to be cooked to feed us.

The second night, at the same place, we had a wet night; the storm came and soaked our tent from the top to the mattress while we were away. Luckily, it was warm enough to enable us to get a reasonable night's sleep. Two nights later, we were camping at another beach further north, and I learnt another lesson, this time with an attack by sand flies. Although we were aware and prepared to defend ourselves, we were not fast enough to avoid the attack, and they had my entire body for their dinner, costing me tears and desperation for at least an hour before I fell asleep exhausted. The lesson was learnt: no more feed for the sand flies from then on.

We had planned to follow the coast up to the beginning of Kimberly Region, but the rain was so heavy that our gear and my personal items were getting wet. We still had to face more rain before we would be able to get there. Listening to the news, we were closely following the forecast path of Cyclone Carlo, which had started to advance towards us. We had to make a little change to our plans, due to the force of nature. We drove all that day and night to get to a safe place where we could wait until the cyclone passed us. It was close to ten o'clock that night before we reached Port Headland and found a caravan park to stay that night. There was no chance to sleep in a tent. The area around was under red alert, waiting for the storm to worsen. That morning, around two o'clock, the winds reached us, considerably mild compared to the centre of the cyclone, but still braking tree branches and flooding the room through the entrance door. It seemed like my heart was used to storms and cyclones. This was a bit different. I remember when I was preparing to leave Brazil.

I was finishing my university course in economics sciences, and all my colleagues from the previous five years were sharing our plans for the future. I was asked about mine, and I said, "I am going to Australia to learn English."

But only I knew; it was a decision made with the speed of a cyclone, pushed by the undermined love affair I was living in, along with the subconscious control of my mother generating the pressure. There was another collection of broken ideals in my career for eight years in an energy company, where I would not be unhappier, having to endure unfair politics and games. I needed to make a turnaround, changing my life to seek meaning and perhaps happiness. In three months' time, I went through my own storm, soaked in tears when sleeping, travelling on my own out of my country's borders for the first time, leaving behind a love affair, which was huge and filled with disappointment after four years of great moments. It had ended in deception, once more making me feel foolish enough to sweep everything away, restarting from the scraps.

I decided to make one stop in Toronto to visit a friend of mine. She was living there with her brother, and I managed to meet her, overcoming the trauma of only being able to speak about fifty English words. My friends would have loved to have me stay in Canada for at least a month for the holidays, but my final destination was Sydney. On that day, I left Toronto at about six in the evening, heading to Australia with a stop in Honolulu, Hawaii.

When the airplane left Toronto, the flight attendants only spoke English and French, which was chaos for my communication skills. I still had my clock on Canada's time zone, and I had never been in more than one time zone, except in my own country, with only a one-hour difference. I was watching my clock go around and around, and there was only night and night. I could not say a word; I just read my books, trying to learn some words in English from a magazine given to me by a guy on the airplane. I think he realised my desperation, but he didn't help me much. I felt like I had been dumped in the abyss without a parachute. After I slept a few times for a total of about six hours each, the airplane landed in Honolulu. The flight schedule required all the passengers to leave the aircraft and wait in the transit room until the flight could resume to its final destination, Sydney. Of course, that was obvious, but I was so desperate that I could not ask a question, not in English or French. So I decided to stay in my seat until I found a way to communicate. A flight attendant approached and asked me, "Do you speak English?" I said no. She said, "Do you speak French?" I said no. She said, "What language do you speak?"

I said, "Portuguese."

She made a signal with her hands for me to wait. I understood her body language and waited until a man in uniform came to me from the cockpit. He introduced himself as a flight engineer and spoke with me in Portuguese.

That was a blessing. I breathed deeply and presented my apologies for the attitude, explaining that I knew what I supposed to do, but the only thing I wanted was to know where I was, what time it was, and how much longer we would be flying. That was the way I found to get help. He smiled kindly and helped me out of the plane, answering my questions. From that time on, we flew until half past seven in the morning, Sydney time. I thought that I was right and there was Sydney's airport. I was 100 per cent sure, and I went to pick up my luggage. There, just standing in front of me, was none other than John Travolta. I said to myself, "Oh my God, where am I? Am I still sleeping? Is it a dream? Am I in America? I am sure that I left for Australia."

I looked at him, and he looked towards me. Of course, I had the scariest smashed face at this time, but I still could not say a word, and I didn't. I picked up my luggage and left, extremely confused, heading to Customs for the next two hours. The Customs agents checked each millimetre of my personal belongings, documents, and body, and I did not have the slightest reaction, even for a second, regardless of the fact of been through this unknown Customs procedure. I was exhausted. When it was all clear they let me go, and I was in Kingsford Airport, inside Australia. I phoned some friends, and they gave me directions, so I was able to get a taxi to take me to their address. My friends then took me to the beautiful Darling Harbour, the icon of the city, and to somewhere riding the ferry boat. At the end of the trip, I was delighted and sleeping like a rock.

My journey to Australia was like a cyclone's passage. I was willing to spend time studying; the feelings I had before takeoff in Sao Paulo, Brazil, were that I would not come back to live in Brazil. The sensation when I was in Australia was like I had died in a big accident, and I was reborn on the other side of the planet. I could even look behind and see the scrap from my personal storm.

After Cyclone Carlo had passed, in the morning we walked over the pieces of trees that were smashed everywhere before continuing our journey to Kununurra. It is a town of eight thousand people, located in the northern part of Western Australia. Here we spent a week repacking before the next part of our journey by land. We stayed in a farmhouse seven kilometres away from the centre of town. It was a very nice place, with lots of green, full of wildlife, such as snakes, wallabies jumping around, ducks, birds, spiders, and many small insects, all happily living at almost fifty degrees Celsius at this time of year. I was able to catch up with my son and some friends left in Perth. After a week, as planned, we were heading to the East States of Australia.

There were a few times in my life when I had huge changes that seemed to happen fast, as to avoid the slow suffering process. The journey I was just beginning seemed to be a huge one, like my arrival in Australia in 1990. I was on my own; I just had one couple as friends, with no relatives and a broken heart to deal with. Despite my plan and my return ticket in thirty days, I had the feeling that I was staying for longer, perhaps for many years.

Not speaking any English was my first priority and the main reason I ventured to Australia. My friends took me to complete my enrolment at an English course which would start eleven days after my arrival. I was also seeking a job, any kind of labouring job to make some money and find a place to stay. Everything ran smoothly; my new good friends were communicating for me until the time I found myself living in a student community house with two Aussies, one person from Japan, two from China, and two from Thailand. Luckily, the house was next door to my friends, and that was a relief. So I was ready to start to move around during my independent living in Sydney's southern suburb of Kingsford.

My first outing to shop for supplies was also my first nightmare. I decided to go to a shopping centre about six kilometres away from home. It was afternoon, and I could see all around at least and be a bit more aware of the surroundings. This would be good and involved even my safety, crossing streets and roads, as I was still automatically looking for cars coming on my right side. I'd never had contact with driving on the left-hand side, but after a few jumps back to avoid motor vehicles, I was soon getting used to it. I took public transport to get to the shopping centre, and it was beautiful, distracting me from my thoughts of loneliness.

Australian people were amazingly helpful and patient in trying to understand my signals, sounds, and body language. My shopping was done, and around five in the afternoon, I decided to return. I took the bus back home and jumped out halfway before I got home. It was a Sunday, and the buses did not pass by often, so it was a long wait before leaving, and it was already dark. I had my shopping bags and found myself completely lost in the deserted street, with no chance to get help. I hadn't realized that could happen, and I was in a very deep, unsolvable circumstance. There was no other thing to do but sit down on the curb and cry with my entire body, soul, and mind. For the first time in my thirty-one years, I realized why kids cry. Before, I thought they just wanted to make a noise. I thought to myself, kids cry because they are feeling something. They are suffering; they are hungry; they are thirsty; they are in pain, cold, hot, frustrated, etc. That was it: *I am like a kid right now, and I am crying for all those things, and at my age I am alive! And I am lost!* It was all because I was like a little baby and could not talk. This was a wake-up call to meet someone who was sleeping inside me, and in one way or another, I had to find it. I survived, when I was absorbed by my discovery and realized a cab was approaching. I signalled it to stop, and I gave him the address, which was less than five minutes away. He kindly drove me back home, and the clock was showing a few minutes past ten o'clock.

Three weeks later, I was about ready to melt—hugely homesick and still heartbroken over the former love relationship; but I was determined not to return to those memories that could make things harder. When I checked my mail, I found a letter from *him*. I had my laundry started, and I was supposed to hang around. It was raining, and I just walked up to the entrance of the laundry and sat with my body half in and half out. I didn't realise the raindrops were pouring over my hands. The writing wasn't impermeable and started to become a stain of blue taking over the paper; I could read just a bit, not more than I was interested in. As the rain washed away those words, it did so with my heart and refreshed my body from those burning memories still remaining in my body. It touched my soul and cuddled me to accept that it was time to let go to discover Australia.

We had another couple thousand miles to get to the east coast, and we still had to go on with short journeys between sunrises and sunsets, each time back on the road with some more writing and reflections.

Chapter Two

Anytime you are filling the now with thoughts about how
you use to be, concerns about what someone has done to
harm you, or worries about the future, you are saying:
"No, thank you" to your Source for this precious gift.
—Dr. Wayne W. Dyer, Excuses Begone!

From My Town to a Metropolitan Area of Fifteen Million People

This morning, we could see that the green grass was really sharing colours with the brownie seeds' spots, announcing the end of the wet season. My memories were about new thoughts, never healed completely. However, at that point, I was able to reflect with more desire to learn and live, rather than suffer and heal; then I dove forward with those thoughts.

I have no other way to start my day than thinking about love. As I used to say to my son, my concept of competition is "never compare and look beside you to evaluate yourself in comparison with others to became better; get inside yourself every evening, and give yourself a few minutes to reflect about what you have done on that day that you really should improve in some way, doing better for yourself and for everyone involved." Do this so you can think about how to improve yourself for the next day and grow naturally at your own pace, and that is also love for yourself.

Once more, I find that love is a great tool to help us when we become surrounded by a kind of competition in life. If we observe, we always will find, in one way or another, someone calling us to that field, even in our personal relationships. I am sure that in this era in which we live, we never stop facing challenges with partnerships and the intrinsic need for competition in one way or another, ending up in a kind of competition over who controls power. I find that my personal concept of competition is the best to stick with. Love, for me, is also freedom and does not have chance to grow if we compete. That would trap us in relationships, and it would become as ephemeral as a night's wind.

These thoughts were already a wheel, steering inside my being, as the circumstances of my life they were challenging. But it was all about finding, knowing, and understanding myself like I never had done.

The east coast was very windy and wet, and we started looking for a yacht since we left Townsville in the northeast. We drove down, heading to Brisbane, stopping and checking every yacht club and marina for brokers and vessels for sailing back to Windham, Western Australia. We finally found the right catamaran for the journey, which happened to be the one Will had contacted by e-mail at the beginning and seemed to be the most suitable.

At four o'clock in the morning, March 16, we woke up, had a cup of coffee, and kept running. We had to be at the mooring of the vessel to go out for the sea trial. Six hours later, we were out of the water at the Brisbane port yard, prepared for the cruise. Will was over the moon with the new toy.

We went back to the caravan park and prepared to move on, to live on *the Vessel* until it was ready to start the sailing journey back. Observing Will's behaviour, I had the feeling more than ever that I should focus myself on the sailing journey, learning all I could to help ensure a safe journey returning to Kununurra by sea. I wanted to enjoy each step and just wait for the biggest adventure I knew that was there for me, as I was stepping into a completely unknown zone of my life.

Thirty-eight days of living in the Brisbane port yard, working on the vessel to prepare it for the journey, wasn't easy. We had a stepladder from the deck down to the concrete deck, which sat another metre lower. The toilets and showers were about thirty metres away from the vessel. We could not use water on board, as we had no way to dispose of it, only for clean use straight out of the hose. We had tradesmen, including an engineer, mechanics, painters, welders, and a handyman coming and going, working to accomplish the list of jobs as Will wished.

I remember that at the end of this period, we had made some friends and had gone out some nights with them, including sleeping over at their house for a break from *Task Fish*. Yes, that was the name we had christened the yacht after a new look and some changes. Some believe that it is not auspicious to change a vessel's name, unless you do so, on hard ground and not in the water, so we were safe of any superstitious beliefs. The name *Task Fish* was chosen because of Will's passion for a special kind of fish, also called black spot tusk fish. It surely would make him feel happy, and that was a good idea. Soon, everyone had forgotten about the old name of the vessel. I confess that I was quite happy too. For me, the new journey should be lighter in memories and history, as we would have enough to write about on our own.

All the last touch-ups were done, and as we were booked for twelve noon, the *Task Fish* was lifted from the hard deck to the water. There she was placed softly by those kind and dedicated guys, one operating and the other spotting around to make sure all would be done well.

I must describe that moment. It seemed to be an ordinary one; however, at that point, I felt like almost jumping out and just leaving, going back home. Then I thought, *Where is home now?* I felt like I had my body as my home and nothing else. Anywhere I went was home, and anywhere I ventured, I would have challenges in the same proportion or even bigger. I had a few minutes on my own, and my inner voice shouted at me, *No way! You are not giving the best time up, are you?*

I was diving fearlessly into the huge transmutation of feelings inside me. Since I ended my marriage, I was trapped in tension and grief, and my sexuality was in first place, making the revolution. My desires were insane; my body's sexual functioning was higher than at any other time in my life. In spite of this, and regardless of the excitement of the journey itself, I could feel peace in my heart. It was all about thinking of being in the part of nature I loved the most: the sea, and being able to heal myself from so much pain. And I felt God within more than ever, like whispering, and touching on my shoulder, softly.

You love the ocean, don't you? So go and sail!

Once more, I was facing the same challenge of faith and an enduring fight with myself, to understand my relationship with my body and my spiritual evolution. There were physical changes due to the "special age" I was living in with my physical body. I was setting myself free from traumas created by my broken marriage. For the last four years, I had been having counselling and personal-development therapy, including spiritual and energy work for holistic healing and balancing techniques. As I was told by my Reiki master eight years before: "Now the books will start to fall from the shelves for you to follow your path." And it did happen, but my body seemed to be later in the process.

My sexuality was simply disturbing me, like a depressive illness pushing me in a very savage way, which I believed had pushed me to my limits. I believe that there is no perfect health system; we have a very good one. I had visited doctors and received annual check-ups. However, it is not about the system. It is about ourselves and the way we know our lives from inside and the way we feel inside. It's about how it comes out and reflects on our physical bodies and on our living environment, society, and so on. I was drawn back to be close to nature in every single sense. I felt that I needed it more than ever to release negativity and to heal. I found myself again heading to God's lap, going to the ocean. And I kept reinforcing to myself:

That is what you came here for, and you are free to go and to stop anytime you feel like; that was the deal. You know what is right for you.

Remember: you are never alone, and you live what you co-create, and you had dreamed it.

That was my inner voice, so *go and sail!*

Is that it? I asked myself, and I felt that was good enough! No experience; any learning!

It was time to turn the boat's ignition on, and we faced the first unexpected problem. It seemed to be too fast to have something not work after all this time, with so many professionals taking care of everything. The motor wasn't responding; we had no current, and the engine could not be started. Will seemed so frustrated and nervous that I thought he would have a heart attack. So I started making phone calls. The electrician came over and jumped on board, and they managed to fix the problem in a few minutes. There was a loose wire left by someone; we did not have a clue who. All was resolved, and we were able to motor for a few metres into the Brisbane River Channel, where we planned to spend two nights before leaving.

We powered the yacht for about twenty minutes and then anchored. Will decided to check inside the motor compartment, and he found another unwanted surprise: the motor compartment was rapidly filling with water. The yacht had to be lifted back to the hard deck again for repairs. There, Will started to see if he could find a way to fix the leak. Checking the water pump, he then went through the switchboard, where the electrician left some wire undone. I didn't find the purpose for those wires, which upon further investigation turned out to be connected to the pump to remove water from the bilge.

Will first fixed the wiring and then was able to turn the pump on, and the water was gradually pumped out of the engine compartment. When the water was pumped out, I could see where it was coming in from. There was a hole where the propulsion leg for the inboard motor was fitted to the hull. Will dove into the water under the yacht and found the hole. Now the problem was how to repair it. The yacht was on the water, and the hole needed to be blocked immediately, before the engine compartment became flooded! It was just prior to a long holiday weekend, so it seemed we would be stuck there until the long weekend finished and those busy contractors became available to make the necessary repairs. The alternative was to undertake the necessary repairs ourselves. I had the idea to use some of the rubber we had on board, cutting something to plug the hole until we had a chance to beach the yacht on some sandy bank, dry up the area surrounding the hole, and close it properly. Another brilliant idea came from Captain Will, who called me and said, "Can you please go to the office desk and grab that stuff I took off the poster on the wall and give to me?"

I said, "What are you talking about?"

"Do you know about that stuff—I don't remember the name—that we use to stick posters on the walls?"

I said, "Yes, it is blue tack."

He said, "That is it."

"Are you crazy?" I said, incredulous. "Are you intending to fix the hole with blue tack?"

He insisted. "Yes, can you bring this to me, please?"

"Okay, but how you can guarantee that we will be safe with that?"

He said, "We have no choice. It is all closed at the port, and we are not going back to the hard deck to fix it." That was his call.

I ran inside the yacht, and there was the little ball of used blue tack on the office desk. I passed it to him, and in a few seconds, the water stopped coming inside the engine compartment. From time to time, I checked personally, and there was no more water by the following morning. The pump was on, and it would automatically turn on and pump the water out anyway. Everything seemed to be fine, and we were prepared to take off anytime from that afternoon on.

The following day was Good Friday. We had arranged with Will's relatives that we would be waiting for them to come over for the farewell, so we stayed one more day to see them. As we prepared to depart from Brisbane Port, everyone was happy, posing for a family picture. They hadn't been together, the mother and the three children, for about twenty years, so that was a very special meeting. They seemed really happy, and so was I. After a few drinks, some pictures taken, laughter and joy, they left, and we just rested until the following morning. At that time, we checked the yacht and our gear, turned the engine on, and cruised out along the Brisbane River towards the sea, and off we went.

Chapter Three

Happiness is like a butterfly; the more you chase it, the more it will elude you, but if you turn your attention to other things, it will come and sit softly on your shoulder ...
—Henry David Thoreau

Good Memories to Overcome Big Challenges

My first challenge came when we were entering the channel between Fraser Island and the shore. It was low tide, and we were caught by five-metre waves breaking in front of and behind the yacht. I found it better to bend my knees, as the yacht was caught by the waves, making movements before any stiffness and panic could ruin my legs and back. It was not a very pleasant feeling, being on a twelve-ton surfboard over breaking waves and sandy banks. I just looked at the water and faced it with no fear. I had nothing else to do until the captain turned the yacht around and started to sail back away from the danger zone. It took only a few minutes, although it felt like long hours. Sometimes nothing is better than not knowing too much, as it seems to be easier to deal with the unknown when you are faithful.

It was not much different than the feeling of arriving in a new country with no knowledge of the language, and you have to move around, earn a living, study, and work for yourself, as I did.

All the suffering of breaking up with the long years of routine and old habits for a completely new culture had been challenging to oneself; the one I was just about to invent, to make reborn. What else could we call these circumstances?

Every night at bedtime, after a new and challenging day, I started to cry. My entire body shook, even the bed, as I thought I would not be able to cope with it all. I asked myself, *why did I decide to do it?* I had finished my university course after five years of full-time studies, finished with the second-best score in my classroom. I had been promoted at my workplace, moved to a new and beautiful place. Everything I had achieved was desired by many and reached by just a few, and I just decided to leave it all behind. It was a push from somewhere we cannot identify, so I just found my own justification. That was it! I was born for challenges and an adventurous life. However, I thought this time I went too far!

My mother used to say, "The best remedy to forget a failed painful love relationship is to find a new love." So I thought about her saying, looked at her love life, and asked myself, *How did she learn that?* She had a married life for fifty-five years with my father. She had only one man in her life and loved only him! In some way, I could feel that what she was saying was very true, even not having experienced it on her own.

Anyway, at this point in my life, I was about to turn over a page with higher achievements, rather than failures. Australia was such a different country for me to discover, enjoy, and learn from. I decided that relationships could wait, as I had other pains to deal with. I went to work in a small factory, making computer cables. I started welding cables and then learned how to test them, packing and attending orders. I spent three months doing stock-taking for the end of the financial year. The job was supposed to be very temporary, as I was covering one permanent employee on holidays; my overseas contract lasted until her return. She returned, and I was asked to work for a few more weeks. The business was about to reduce staff, but on that specific week, the orders were many, and they needed to attend to them soon, so I agreed to keep working until it was finished. I met Hild, the employee I was covering for, and we started a friendship, also exchanging language skills, as she was from a different language background.

One afternoon, I spoke up about my stress from homesickness and the lack of physical exercise. I used to play volleyball, go jogging, and visit a gymnasium. Since my arrival in Australia, I was stuck with no physical activities, so she promptly proposed that we go play tennis. I had never played tennis before; neither was she very skilled, so she said, "I have a good friend who is patient and plays fair, and he would be happy teaching us. If you would like to, I will arrange it for us."

So I happily accepted, and we would go after work the following week. I was very excited with the idea to do something physical for fun; I couldn't wait for the day to come. She stopped over at my house to pick me up, and off we went. After less than two months in Australia, I was already attending English classes after work and had met one guy who was unable to speak my language, just as I couldn't speak his. Anyway, it didn't click, and we just saw each other twice and that was all; nothing else happened. Just a few times out with friends for dancing, a few drinks, and that was my life, with my focus on learning English.

That was May, and there we were, pretty comfortably dressed for the first tennis class. It was not too hot for tights and a long-sleeved T-shirt. When we arrived at the tennis court, I saw two guys playing. My eyes caught the older one, and he immediately smiled; I felt my knees loosen. From that moment on, we shook our legs together for the next eighteen years of marriage. My husband friends used to say that was a payback to Hild, as she was introduced to her husband twenty years before by the same friend she was introducing to me, who became my husband.

A new phase of my life was about to be unfold, and again like a fool, I thought everything would be more than new. I already had the challenge of speaking English and learning about English culture. At the same time, I entered into a marriage with a man who was used to speaking a language other than English. I prefer to follow the view of Dr. Wayne Dyer, when he says everything has a spiritual explanation.

Eighteen months later, we were flying out of Australia on our honeymoon, passing by Singapore and heading to Italy, Germany, Brazil, and finally Argentina, for a new life beginning.

Chapter Four

*For beautiful eyes, look for good in others; for beautiful
lips, speak only words of kindness; And for poise, walk
with the knowledge that you are never alone.*
—Audrey Hepburn

No Fear Looking Back and Seeking for Myself

Photo by Francisca Lopes

At the beginning of my thirty-second year, I was called to pay attention to my background again, related to the way I was brought up. I was marrying someone with a very different background, from a hugely different culture, a man who was fourteen years older than me and had different beliefs. I was exhaling joy and physical appeal and completely lonely on the opposite side of the planet, missing my friends and relatives so much, but I was hungry for a new life, to get closer to myself in every sense that I could discover. I can say that if I looked back today, I would say the same as I did twenty years afterwards, if asked about that experience. I cannot make any assumptions about anything that is unknown for me. I will do these things and then tell you if they scared me. My question again is: How can you fear something you don't know?

Many times during my life as a student, I walked alone around midnight in a city with the fourth-highest population on the planet. I can remember like yesterday's memories the fragrance of flowers coming from I don't know where. I just knew I was in the company of a big ghost, protecting me in that concrete jungle. Walking back home after spending a long four hours sitting in the classroom would be good exercise, but also very risky and dangerous. However, my steps were always firm and confident. I would say that would be a proper metaphor for my marriage.

There were four years of family, financial, economic, cross-cultural, business, and parenthood experiences, which gave me enough to enjoy my stay while living in Buenos Aires, Argentina's capital. I cannot deny that I found good friends to keep in my heart for eternity. I still miss them very much. However, that country's energy never clicked with mine. In this case, just describing values and people's mentality could fall into unfair judgement, considering that the unique state of consciousness really makes the nation and its people.

Once again in my life, I was living in the middle of a society with strong religious beliefs, observing how it was being a wife, an independent woman, while at the same time being in a environment still undefined for me. We had lived for four years between Argentina and Brazil, since my son was born. We had tried overcoming huge economic changes in both countries. It became both crucial and impossible to survive with any business or employment in the middle of the transition from hyperinflation to stabilization of the economic system. Not enough time for adjustments and adaptation made my husband and I feel unfit.

We decided to travel back to Australia, to restart all over again. We were also planning to be in Australia for the Olympic Games in 2000, so we started packing. It was another heartbreaking time for me and my family; now with one more to be included as part of the living family. Just turning five years old, my son was travelling to his new home for the first time. Regardless of being used to travel and already speaking Portuguese and Spanish, and always having been surrounded by love, he had his new, big challenge with another language: English.

We arrived back in Sydney in 1998, and in less than two weeks, he started at school. I remember the first time I dropped him at school. He was just hugging my legs, as he was pulled by his teacher, who was saying to me, "Just leave." I turned my back to hide my tears, listening as his crying faded behind my back. He tried to escape from school and was caught by school staff for two days. Afterwards weekend followed that, on the following Monday at five o'clock in the morning, he awoke throwing up, and I knew he was under stress, so I asked him, "Would you like to stay home?"

He said, very proudly, "No, Mom. I don't want to miss class."

And from that day on, he was okay. We had a few issues to adjust with his behaviour, due to cross-cultural living, but it was sorted easily. Again, there was intrinsically the physical and "something else," all sorts of things related to our beliefs, culture, and the way we are brought up. Since early school days, we experience the living world of our physical and spiritual side. My son experienced the education of both Saxon and non-Saxon roots in his earlier schooling.

We are seated in between three background roots here, with three different stories. We are neither of Latin nor Saxon background. We are a mixed cultural background, with native Indian, plus African, plus European Latin background predominantly, through more than five hundred years of history. So surely it will be a specific concept of "hands on and hands off." That was a little challenging for him.

This is one thing that we always had to deal with and still count on some aspects, concern about our mixed background and living in Australia, and also dealing with sexuality. I found it controversial, as in our culture, we had the most preconception, restricted, and controlled social behaviour, grounded by a society formed with high influence from religious beliefs concerning sexuality.

We are a very tactile people, by which I mean we touch others with our hands, with no sexual intention. Living in the opposite cultural background, it sometimes shocks us. This experience was huge for me, and having to learn it was a big push to my journey in seeking answers involving faith, spirituality, and sexuality. Living this, for me, was my way to discover humankind's evolution. For a kid, it is not an easy task either, living between both cultures, where one of the first rules at school is "hands off"; back to our roots, kids don't play by those rules, and they learn the meaning of touching in a different way. The rules that show us touching as either sexuality-related or fight-related are painful for us, as we also touch with love, respect, and warmth, regardless of sexual desires.

That is a crucial point to understand and feel that God would never be a part of sexuality for any grounding of pure human values created to facilitate and please to some, in exchange for others' pain and disgrace. I would say that my son and I had a great privilege to have experienced and lived with three different cultures in the most important part of our lives. We still had time to learn more and grow fairly, without having to harm others on our own mediocrities.

I still have choking situations, and sometimes I feel how little I know about human behaviour, based on my practical living. However, I can clearly feel the peace I found to face anything, just coming across those few years of my life. (Yes, I say *few years,* because I believe and can feel the eternity.) So I am able to say how lucky I am, and anyone can be seeking evolution of self in life.

May 12: During the latest days, we had sailed and planned to arrive in Yeppoon, a beautiful, hilly town, located about four hundred nautical miles north of Brisbane. My dearest friend Chiss used to live there and was waiting for us, for a few days' sailing with us. We would catch up and enjoy some fishing together around the Capel Islands.

A few minutes after noon, we were anchoring, scouted by dolphins at the entrance of Rosalyn Bay. We spent a week, supplying and looking for the best time and day for taking off. Chiss took her boyfriend with her, and so we had a nice time, staying and celebrating friendship and good times together, with one little mistake. The drink didn't match with the weather, and I felt very sick for another few weeks. There was no time to stay on land to recover, and I didn't want to. I was focussed and sticking to the plan of sailing. I already had the insight that it would only be a sailing business trip.

It turned hard for me, as I had developed certain feelings for Will. It should sound good for the journey, but nothing could be harmful to my relationship with the ocean and my own self. We also had a strong and respectful sense of companionship, with more likes in common than dislikes. The trip still could be promising.

We managed to take some pictures, and on the last day in Yeppoon, I felt the same sensation of emptiness and the wish to stop, and I felt again the wish to go back home, but once more, I felt that home was my body, in the now, where else it would be. So I just felt like printing the pictures, sending them to my son and relatives overseas, and not looking back.

Now we had the same routine for the sailing and working all adjusted. Every night before bed, we had a meeting to plan the next day's trip. If we would anchor in any river's mouth, we would go crabbing; if there was a beach with rocks, we would have oysters; if we would anchor in a reef or island, we would go reef fishing. And of course, we would face those odd days with rough waters and strong winds sometimes against us, making it impossible to do any real sailing. Sometimes we faced real hardship out there, such as facing winds of forty to forty-five knots, blowing us anywhere. We managed to save ourselves from dangerous situations, winding the sails in and controlling the vessel without harm. The tropical area of the Queensland Coast was for us the hardest part to sail.

All the compensation was my free time spent on the deck, appreciating life. I was living and harmonising with the waters, land, forest, rocks, sun, sunrises, sunsets, and stars, and it was all priceless.

Here I am again, sitting on this deck. I cannot see land in front of my eyes; they are full of light-green waters and sunlight. The sea is calm; there is just a blow of wind, so calm that our speed is around four knots. The plan for today is to navigate around sixty nautical miles and anchor at one island. No better moment to turn within myself and meet my inner child. I can see in my mind that beautiful girl, blue eyes, sometimes so depressed, crying, dirtying her face, scrubbing her dirty hands all around her eyes, trying to dry her tears. And I cannot avoid the images of her playing in a small mountain of sand in front of the main door; so little, so lonely. It is not easy, but in my mind, I literally called her: *Come with me and sit on my lap, please, come!*

Now we can see together. Let me wrap my arms around you and keep you safe. Let us see together far away the beautiful and magnificent little bit of our spaceship, Mother Earth.

The vessel is bouncing slowly, sliding over the waters in a magical way, and we cannot take our eyes away from the waters just here now. Dolphins come and swim, as if asking us beautifully to play with them under our feet. Let's dive with them in our dreams and in our hearts!

It is so peaceful that we can feel the freshness of the water reaching our skin, and that is amazing. Let's seal the deal here to meet again. Let's open our hearts and love each other as we never did and play, sailing together, and help each other to find answers while we play and relax. Let's put all together: the entire family, bringing us all to this journey, as we can do in the real world: adults and children around the table to celebrate life. And before I come back to my sailing day, I will recite some words I wrote for my son, as the wish of having him with us now as in my thoughts and in my heart:

It is amazing …
To look at you walking,
And each step showing firmly
A brave move loving.
It is amazing
To look at you when you are smiling

33

And feel your heart beating kindly.
It is amazing
To feel your arms hugging
And your love pouring.
It is amazing
To see your body waving
When you are dancing
And your soul flowing softly.
It is amazing
Here when you're singing
With your voice vibrantly.
It is amazing
To hear you suspire sweetly
When you are sleeping
And your lips resting serenely.
It is amazing …
To fall deeply
With you into your dreams

There were unforgettable moments gathering together my essence and one of the other most loving parts of me, which was my son.

We learn that we love our children, teach them how to fold their socks nicely and tidily, each pair accordingly. They love to see it done; however, at some point in their lives, we think that we are no longer needed. But if we put their socks unpaired and loose in their drawer, they will wear one black and one white with the same love and joy. There is no bad way to love.

I am ready for the day, and I know I carry in my being this beneficial kiss of the waters to cheer me up to the next encounter.

A week later: I finished my morning duties and decided to throw myself into my reading berth, as the day looked like rain, and we had only a few hours to go before we could anchor, according to our plan for the day. I questioned myself about something I would never forget in my life, and that was one of those painful experiences that take a long time to accept.

Chapter Five

Before God we are equally wise—equally foolish.
—Albert Einstein

The tragic ending of a love story and kindness

I was in my early forties and still attending classes to improve my language and skills. In my spare time, I was teaching Portuguese to a guy I met at his second-hand furniture shop. His name was Billy, and he was very keen to learn, as he had been in Brazil nine years before and still had a friend living there. He used to live with his girlfriend, Lenny, and we became friends. One day, he called me and said, "Listen, I have a friend from Brazil, and his partner just arrived with an eight-year-old daughter, so I thought that maybe you would like to meet her. She is a bit lost; her daughter still doesn't speak English. You can have your son's on the go to help her with the language, and she seems very friendly. Her name is Helen. Would you allow me to give her your number to call you or be in touch with her?"

I said, "Okay. If you want to give me her number, I'll contact her. I am happy with that."

So he gave me her number, and I contacted her to arrange to meet. I invited her and her family over for a meal. Everything seemed to be smooth, and the girl was happy. Her partner, Enyo, and her daughter, Nelly, also seemed to be happy. They came to study language for a short term, and it would be useful for them to receive any tips on settling themselves and get a bit of support for her life change. It would not be hard at all to spend time in her company, as she really was special. Coincidence or not, she was also a very spiritual person, so we clicked straight away as friends. I was preparing my son's birthday party, and she promptly offered a hand with everything she could. He was also good at cooking and seemed to enjoy helping with his cooking skills.

We became good friends. She was confident about her life and told me living in Brazil, she used to be a bilingual secretary in a multinational company. She had a beautiful house there with a swimming pool that she left for rent, and she was the daughter of a two-sibling family.

One day I asked her, "Why did you decide to come to Australia?"

She said, "Because Enyo and I have been together for about eighteen months. There, things were not going very well; he came first, and he was missing our being together. I also had a bad experience while I was there on my own. My house was broken into by men who held guns to our heads. I was very traumatized by so much violence and thought that I could come, have my English improved. Also, Nelly could learn a bit of English, which will serve her in her future. So we decided to have a life change here. According to my mother, I was very courageous, coming with him under these circumstances, across the planet with my daughter. She found that I should be more cautious with him. But you know, when we still have some feelings left, we want to try to make things better anyway, and that was what I thought. It all came to me like it would be a life experience!"

She seemed happy with the move. Sometimes I try to describe her, and I still cannot find the words for something I used to observe about her. When we walked down the street and there were two men walking and talking as they passed us, they used to stare breathlessly at her in an unexplainable way, and she would say, "That was for you!" I would see straight away that they were looking at her and not at me. It was very common, and we always would end up laughing.

She didn't seem to be a model type that men look at in the streets, definitely not. She was shorter than the average considered pattern of beauty, and her skin was covered with freckles. She never wore anything extravagant, didn't have big boobs or a big behind. She had a shapely body, neither too skinny nor overweight. She had long, curly hair like threads of gold, and she had the most beautiful smile. It was special on her face, and it used to make her look like an angel. She was about thirty-eight years old.

I was doing part-time work and part-time studies, so we didn't have too much time. That summer, we would make the most of our spare time, going to the beaches, even for a few hours at a time. She confessed to me that she was not happy with her relationship and she was trying to break up. However, Enyo was inflexible and was unhappy with the way she was being treated. So we talked and I told her she should be mindful of her safety and look for help if she felt she needed it.

She used to say, "There is nothing that we cannot solve with a good talk. I prefer to do it this way."

We were in a good friendship, and we knew we would be there for each other, doing what we could do, even just a requested phone call.

A few weeks later, on a Thursday, I arrived back home after school, and she turned up perplexed. I called her inside, encouraged her to calm down, and asked what it was all about. She mumbled, stating that she found he was planning to leave a week before and had given notice to their real estate agent to end the lease.

He left her a note saying that she should sell his car and keep the money. He left the apartment bonus letter signed, which would expire the following day. He cancelled her card from their Brazilian join account, and he took around five thousand dollars from her house's money. His car would be worth around five hundred, and the bonus another eight hundred. The furniture was less than one thousand. I asked her what she had done and what it would be like for her and her daughter; but she did not take any action. She just knew that she should leave the apartment by the following Saturday morning.

I explained to her that she would still stay in the apartment. However, if it was me, I would feel safer moving to a different place. I offered that she could stay with my family until she sorted things out.

She said, "I believe that he left the country, so I will stay there."

I said, "If you want to stay with us with your daughter and find a different place to move to, you are welcome."

But she insisted on sorting things out over the weekend, as she found it was the way. She decided to stay, and we could only support her. She seemed devastated but always kind and very strong at the same time.

The weekend was her chance to recover, at least a little bit, from that terrible event, but in some way, she felt she should trust that it would help her with the breaking-up process. She believed she would have relief and time to decide what to do next.

The weekend went by too fast to change much. She was home early Monday, before Nelly's school started. Enyo was knocking on her door. She was strong enough to tell him that she hadn't called the police for the unfair deal, one more of his deals that was triggering her depression and her collection of disappointments, as she used to admit and show me the proof. However, he wasn't welcome back anymore. She showed him that she no longer had room for him, as she settled the second bedroom for shared accommodations. He tried to make up with her, but she asked him to keep to his plan and travel away, as he said he would, in the note he left.

He turned around and left.

Enyo, before he came to Australia and before he met Helen, was an engineer in a multinational company. He had been married and divorced twice, with three children. He had dusky skin and was taller than average; he used to attend the gym often, to keep himself well presented and fit. He seemed to be very proud of his skills and himself, whereas she was humble and caring, down-to-earth, centred, and a naturally happy person.

He went to the United States, passing by Canada, and finally to Brazil. While he was travelling, he used to call her from where he was. She told me he would not let her sleep, phoning her many times, waking her up, as he was thinking strongly of her. She used to say that he was very powerful mentally, and she was like an open channel. He knew, and he was always in contact with her.

Enyo would not give things up easily, and he was always trying to convince Helen that this time, everything would be different, and he would change his behaviour. He said he'd had a wakeup call, travelling with a pastor who had counselled him enough to make things different. Nelly, at this time, was completely supportive of her mother in her decision not to accept him back, as she was not happy with the way he used to deal with her. But he knew her weak points and bought her presents that she was dreaming about. He gave Helen perfume, clothing, jewellery, and beauty products. She came to visit me to give me the latest news. I asked her, "What are you going to do?"

She said, "I am firm on my decision, and this time Nelly is with me, so we won't receive him back. I'll convince him to keep going on with his life and let us do the same."

I asked her, "Where are you going to have your conversation with him? Are you going to meet him in a public place, only you and him?"

She said, "No, I'll talk to him over at my place, and I am happy and convinced that we will have him away from us permanently."

I said, "I really hope you are right and everything goes fine for you all."

That day, she left with confidence. I was happy for her strength and would support her again and again. We can be friendly, offer help, offer a shoulder, and stand by each other as good friends, but we cannot make decisions for our friends, and that was her decision.

Again and again would not be enough. The two girls were happy and confident in their decision to say no. They believed he would walk away and leave them alone forever, but they didn't expect that he had used all his talents and cleverness, based on things he thought would help him to get back to them once more.

He came back, as he had said, and went to see Helen and Nelly. Helen, as usual, in her polite manner invited him inside the house, still confident, and let him start. He approached with gestures of kindness, with hugs and kisses. He had been missing both of them very much and expressed his apologies in person, bringing out of his cases many presents for Helen. Finally he brought out the gift Nelly had been dreaming of for so long: a pair of rollerblades, the latest model, beautiful and expensive. Nelly was completely moved by the surprise gift of her dreams.

Enyo could not have picked a better moment to ask his lover for a second chance. He did so in a tone of deep regret for everything he had caused them. Before Helen could say a word, Nelly jumped to her mother and said, "Please, Mother, give him a second chance!"

He added, "Everything will be different this time, and I will start a new life. To prove it to you, we will go join the church and start to be devoted to our relationship!"

Helen felt trapped for the moment, and she had no other reaction than to say yes and give everyone a second chance.

My next-door neighbour happened to be the pastor of the church they decided to start to attend. As soon as she could, she phoned me to give me the latest news. From that day on, she was really involved in making things work for them. That was more than fair for everyone, a break to see how the moving would impact their lives.

I was also busy with my life, so I hadn't noticed that about three weeks had passed without hearing from Helen. I thought that this time she was happy, as she hadn't either turned up or phoned me until that day. She said that things were not working as promised, and all the same behaviours and deals had returned, so she was not feeling well. First of all, I suggested she go see her doctor for her well-being. I started to keep in touch with her again, to follow up and try to cheer her up again.

The following week, she called and asked to see me after I finished work, as she was home and not feeling well. I finished my work and ran to her apartment. Her daughter was at school, and Enyo was at work. She had thrown herself onto the couch, falling apart, and she seemed completed depressed.

When I arrived, she asked me to come in and pointed me to the table immediately and said, "I cannot cope with this relationship any longer. Please read this letter."

She passed me a letter me a letter he wrote her that said:

I love you, I always will love you, and I know that our lives will be perfect if you accept my love and we will build our lives together. I know you love me, and you and I belong together.

Falling in tears, she said, with her eyes showing the deepest sadness I have ever seen on her face, "I don't love him anymore, and he doesn't accept that. Every time I try to explain it to him, he refuses to listen. I see no future for us anymore, and it is killing me inside. What am I going to do, my friend?"

I held her hand and felt her shaking and suffering profoundly. I thought to myself, *How hard this is, and how lovely she is and how joyful. What an experience she has been through.* I said, "What about going and seeing your doctor again, speaking out word by word? She will help you to a better solution for you. I trust her, and I trust you. You are moved by love, and you will find the best way to sort things out for you. I can go with you, or I can give you ideas. With my heart, I want to see you happy again, smiling, like when I met you. But it is all up to your decision, and I will support you with anything I can do to help."

I suggested to her, "Would you like to organize a week's break and go somewhere to relax, get away, and think a bit more? We could organize it with Nelly's friend's family." I was sure we could do it with no problems, but she thought she would have to try to convince him and go ahead with the break-up for once, just agreeing on seeing her.

She seemed a bit better afterwards, after a cup of relaxing tea. So I left her house, also with my heart tied, but with mild relief.

The following week, she phoned me about the doctor's visit, and she seemed a bit more optimistic and asked for help. She convinced Enyo, and he agreed to move out and set up his own place. However, he said he had no time to look for an apartment and asked for her help.

I couldn't believe it, and it was hard to contain my frustration. But how could I decline helping her? She seemed to have achieved a lot, and I wanted to help her on her way but not make decisions for her. And there we went.

I took her to a few places where I had connections with real-estate agents. We found a few options for lease, and she phoned Enyo to show up for the inspection. I still was with her when he arrived that afternoon. He looked normal, just a normal person coming back from work. I said hello to him and left them to go for the inspection. That unit turned out to be the one he leased. She was phoning me every afternoon for the follow-up, and she seemed to get her spirit back in doing things, even getting involved in a meeting for beautician direct-sales products that week.

She seemed to be happy with each step she was taking according to his requests for help: first finding the unit, then helping with the cleaning, then furnishing and buying appliances, then doing grocery shopping, and *then* he would move! I couldn't believe each time she would say to me how things were running. But there was nothing I could do, other than listen to her and stay with her to the final lap of the run.

He moved into his new apartment on the weekend, and she seemed to be very relieved and happy with her achievement. She called me with the news and said, "Do you remember when I said that it would be better on this way?" She meant *peaceful,* and she was confident that she would achieve this that he would get on with his life, and that this time, things really seemed to be working as she planned.

So I asked her if he had given her his copy of the key for the main entrance. She said he had not yet, but she was about to ask him to bring it over. I insisted she do so, for their safety.

On Monday, she phoned me, saying that she had arranged to see Enyo in the neighbourhood for coffee, and he would bring her the keys. Helen's voice sounded calm and joyful, and she was reaffirming her achievement, hopeful for a new life with her daughter, a very new beginning for her.

That night, I had a dream about her, and in the morning I was very tense about that dream, so I phoned her and said, "How are things going with you?"

She replied, "I am good, feeling relieved. You sound worried."

I said, "I had a dream about you last night, and I didn't like what I felt."

"What was it about?"

I said, "I could not see a clear picture, but I saw a tall, blond guy who I don't know. He seemed Aussie, very kind, but the feeling has nothing to do with him, and I just saw him. The feeling was about you, and it was tense and very much like suffering, in agony. But I cannot describe more than that."

She laughed and said, "I am sorry, my friend, but this time you are wrong. I feel that I am getting my life back, and I am really feeling very good."

Then I asked her, "Who do you think the blond, blue-eyed guy is?

She replied, "Maybe its Dan. He is a friend of ours, and he fits your description."

"But do you have any business to sort with him?" The question just came naturally, with no intention to associate things.

She said, "No, he is just a new friend, and we, Enyo and I, met in a restaurant, through another couple about a month ago. But he is just a friend of a friend. I haven't told anything about him to you, because he really is not that close or around since we met. He is the only man I know that matches the guy you saw in your dream, and he invited me for coffee."

I said, "I don't know. You take good care of yourself. Now you need to relax in your new life."

She said, "Don't worry, I will. I will concentrate on my life's plans, do my studies, and have a break. I still need to see my doctor for my stress and depressive treatment, so I don't want any more things to bother me for now. We only need to do the orders for the beautician's meeting, so I'll call you and catch up."

She closed with, "I am afraid this time you are wrong."

I said, "I hope so as well. That was just a weird feeling. Take care."

On Wednesday, two days later, Helen called me to say that she had coffee with Enyo, he gave her the key, and everything was fine. She also commented that Enyo seemed to be okay.

On December 13, I went school and a few hours on my part-time job. We were all busier at this time of year, and things seemed to be under the most normal circumstances for everyone. I arrived home around four in the afternoon and checked my answering machine. She had left a message there for me, saying, "Hi, friend. If you get home before four thirty, can you please give me a call, as I am leaving for my doctor's appointment? Otherwise, I will call you when I get back home or tomorrow. Bye!"

I was just in time and dialled her land-line number first. It was busy, so I tried her mobile number, which was also busy. I tried a few more times but got no answer, so I called another friend. Chiss and I were talking, and suddenly my friend said, "What is going on here?"

I yelled back to her, as I felt the biggest shake inside me and goose bumps, "What happened, Chiss? I felt something horrible too!"

She said, "You know my dining room. All the windows are closed, no wind current or anything around. I am sitting in one of the chairs, and the other one moved like something has pushed it and fell back."

I said, "Check the door. Are you sure that it happened? How? Why?"

Chiss replied, "I swear that is exactly as I described, and I don't know what is happening here. What about you?"

I said, "I don't know! I just felt goose bumps and a strange feeling for a second, but now I am okay. It is all normal here."

We kept up our conversation for a few more minutes and then hung up.

I tried to call Helen back once more, but both of her numbers were busy. I figured she was making some calls for the orders, as she was so enthusiastic and seeking to keep herself busy. We could talk the following day.

It was December 14, and my workplace had booked a Christmas dinner for the employees. Helen's friend was my co-worker, and we used to see each other only at our regular work meetings. They used to live about three blocks away from each other, while I used to live about a half hour's drive away, in the northwest area. Lyn, Helen's friend, had a daughter the same age as Nelly, and they attended the same school. Later, I finished the few hours of work I had scheduled on that day. I thought, *I am not sure if Lyn is going for dinner. I'll call her. It would be nice to see her again.*

I dialled her number. God knew what I was about to hear. Lyn answered the phone, and I asked, "How are you, Lyn?"

She couldn't speak normally, under such shock as she was. Straight away, she said: "You don't know what happened to Helen, do you?" Without stopping to breathe, she added, "She was murdered yesterday. Enyo killed her and killed himself afterwards."

I'd never heard such news in such a way in my life. I was in shock, and I wasn't sure if I wanted to know anything else about what was going on. But Lyn just kept telling me things, one after another, about everything she was aware of. So I asked, "Where are they? Did you see her?"

She replied, "I had Nelly with me, so she could go and see her doctor yesterday; she hadn't turned up to pick Nelly up. I was worried, but I didn't want to alarm the girl, so I decided I should keep the girl with us for the night, and then we went over to her house in the morning. We started to feel worried when Nelly and I saw her tiara on the floor. We entered through the security door, as we had Nelly's keys, and went upstairs. We tried to open the door with the keys; then we found the door locked from inside. We knocked on the door and could not hear anything, so we called the police. They came over. Nelly was so upset! We waited downstairs until the cops could get into the apartment, and she was there, covered in blood, beaten to death."

She completed the history, as she had already heard from the news that his car was found beside a freeway, one hundred kilometres from her house, at about five in the afternoon. He had his suitcase, travel ticket, and passport to leave the country. His body was in pieces, as he had thrown himself under a truck passing on the freeway, close to where his car was parked.

I had heard enough; I had to hang up. The only thing I wanted to do at this point was to listen to her voice on my answering machine, because I could not accept this tragedy. I refused to believe what was happening; it could not be true. I wished that maybe it was a nightmare, and I wished I could wake up and be relieved. I had to go for counselling immediately, to help me to cope with the situation. I also had detectives phoning me all the time, to go and give my statement as soon as I could.

Billy, Dan, Lyn, another couple I hadn't met, and I were the closest people on her list, so they had to count on our statements to help in the investigation in the case. The Social Security and Brazilian authorities should arrange to send Nelly to her father and family, back to Brazil. That was all the detectives wanted, to put the pieces together. So ten days later, I spent a few hours giving my statement at the police department, focussing on the help to send the girl back to her loved ones soon.

My thoughts always were of how sweet she was. She was a goddess, anytime in any circumstance, with her compassionate gestures for all. She always seemed to be understanding and joyful, a devoted mother, always seeking to give the best to her daughter. She was helpful, friendly, and patient. She was spiritual and always liked to talk about our human evolution in a spiritual way. She seemed to be free from inside, and she was a great giver.

She used to say that she wasn't in love with him any longer, because of the differences and disappointments in their relationship. However, she used to say, "I love him as a human being, and I want him to be happy, with someone else. I just want my life back."

She trusted him all the way, up to the point that she exposed herself fearlessly and for her way to love and give.

We had less than two years of friendship. It seemed too short. However, from the time we met to the present day is more than ten years, and I can still feel her unconditional way to love.

Chapter Six

You should take comfort from the fact that you have enormous potential in reserve if you ever need it.
—Bradley Trevor Greive

The Healing Miracle

On June 15, the plan for the day was to sail twenty nautical miles to reach Hinchinbrook Island, located off the southeast coast of Queensland.

That was a critical time for Will and me for the purposes of our trip. In our personal relationship, we were in conflict, and once more I needed to work on focussing back on sailing purposes. I had given him my word that we would be anchoring the vessel in Windham before the wet season begins. It was hard work for me, but exciting too. Will and I were fortunate to point ourselves to common likes, such as fishing, sailing, and enjoying nature with each mile and under any condition. We managed to find a safe and quiet place to anchor for the night after sailing through twenty-knot winds, which was exciting and pleasant. At the islands, we would look for oysters. Anchoring at low tide, we would have enough time to jump out of the vessel and drive the dinghy to the beach to have some fresh oysters for dinner.

I wasn't the cleverest at taking oysters off the rocks. We each used a normal screwdriver and hammer, and a small container, where we could just have a portion allowed for our meal for that time. Sometimes the tide would not give us enough time, but we could always get what we needed. But that day, I injured the back of my left hand against a rock on another oyster's shell. I was badly cut and bleeding a lot. I washed my hand with the shallow tide water, trying to stop the bleeding until I could reach the first-aid kit on board *Task Fish*. I held the cut with my right hand and ran back after the oysters. The cut was quite deep, but luckily, it didn't affect any nerve or bone badly. It became painful and swollen, making my hand look like half a ball. There was no chance to get to any hospital, so I thought, *I have to handle it,* and I started with my energetic healing process, as we had to keep going.

Three days later, everything had gone miraculously; however, I was not counting 100 per cent on that hand's ability to move around and do my work. I twisted my back jumping out of the dinghy, injuring my sciatic nerve, and then I was in bad shape. We had to stop on the next river anyway, for some more rest and a few things for the following week's supply. So I was able to stay for just one week, doing some isometric exercises and healing. We still would not have any chance to get to a hospital.

I believe that there will always be a higher purpose beyond the ordinary, regardless of our understanding. So stopping my physical body for a while would be a chance for me to pay a bit more attention to my other bodies.

Imagine a good time to reflect and bring to mind things that are sleeping and need to be touched. What is the first thing that comes up? Let's think about relationships. It is a great time to ponder and to understand. My marriage was a kind of relationship that anyone could bet would last forever. Neither my son's father nor I would expect that life would lead to the breakup of our relationship. But there was a need for someone to give the first push on it, to have the way opened for happiness again. I have no regrets related to the time we spent together. I would say that I gave my family the best time of my life, from my thirties to my fifties, if it wasn't for my state of mind afterwards. I understood that life is comprised of many great times, starting when we are born until we find the challenge, face it, overcome it in one way or another, and jump to the next journey. We just have to deal with those "in-between" phases giving us sadness, grief and loss, and fear of new things. I consider myself a gifted person, with the ability to be fooled and always be able to love and trust again and again.

I still remember like it was yesterday. I was speaking with my sister on the phone. She was overseas, and she asked about all the family's health, as usual, and I said to her, "It is all fine; just waiting for a doctor's visit for your brother-in-law. He's having some little clots of blood in his urine sometimes, but he is waiting for an appointment to see what is going on."

We still, at this point, had to be on a waiting list to see a specialist and have a one-day procedure at the public hospitals for check-ups and minor surgeries, so we could not do very much but wait.

My sister just let go some words, like Earth angels do, saying, "Be aware with those signals, as we had experienced with a friend of ours that had the same symptoms and died three months later."

After we finished our phone conversation, I had those words on my mind and could not rest until I called the hospital. On the line, like a miracle, was a nurse's assistant for his specialist, so I just asked, "Will we be watching him die on the waiting list?"

Just like that, the words came from my mouth, without my knowing much about anything. We were just about to check it up. It was senseless, as there was a follow-up from his doctors since a few years ago, but it was always to be just a follow-up. We never had any suspicion that there was anything harmful to his life. But after that phone call, one week later, we received a letter for the one-day surgery procedure, during which a micro-camera would be placed inside my husband and see his bladder.

The day of the procedure, we were there at admission time with all the paperwork done. The examination would normally take thirty minutes, but he didn't come out after a few hours and had to be in the nurses' station to recover from the anaesthetics afterwards. I was there with him, and I felt that every professional coming to see him was looking at me with a weird and invisible sympathy, like looking at a prospective widow. At the end of that day, his registered doctor said, "I want to see you in one week at my surgery, so we can talk about all the results of the tests."

He was discharged, and we went home. A week later, we were back to see his doctor, and we did not spend long in the waiting room. We were all very suspicious, as it usually took very long. But it seemed that they were in a hurry this time, and it was not a good omen.

We were sitting in front of the doctor's desk. She was a young doctor and seemed to be very confident and prepared to give my husband's diagnosis. She started by saying, "We have the results of your tests, and we already arranged a plan for you. You have a very nasty and fast-growing carcinoma tumour on your bladder, and we have planned for you three months of chemotherapy and major surgery, removing your bladder. We will give you a 40 per cent chance of surviving."

That was like a bomb on our heads. I looked at his face, and he was sweating and pale like a blank sheet of paper. So I held his hand and said to him, "Do you believe that you can make it?"

Confused and very stressed, he said, "Yes I do."

"So God can give you the other 60 per cent, and you will make it," I said. "So just believe that you can do it, and trust that God will help us through, and you will be fine."

We went back home, with no more words. We were devastated by the news; we did not want to talk, drink, or eat, just think.

The first few nights, we could not sleep. We were walking around the house, trying to digest it all. We didn't want to talk to many people about it. We just wanted to understand what was happening to us. My son was twelve years old, and I thought he would not understand either, so we restricted it to our thoughts and started to follow the doctor's instructions.

I wrote a poem. That was the way I found at this time to express my feelings and the way I could assimilate things so I could keep myself with the same positive thinking, and faithfully give my husband the support he needed. I went very deep inside my being, and I really felt strength coming from somewhere to accomplish that journey. I was being prepared for that, even if I had not realized it yet.

Everything was darkness:
In the moment when my heart was silent:
We started to look our insight,
We could not find light …
Everything was darkness …
When a golden light brighter than everyday sunlight,
It sprouts from that darkness, as a flashing shining sword.
There was no more doubt.
There was no more illusion.
There was no more pain, because there was no more: neither day nor night
There was only one new sunrise!

Photo by Andrew Stafford

We had been living in Perth since 2004, and my husband was, for the first time in his life, unable to work, as he had an accident working for the mining company. That was the premier intent, to work in the westerns, and on his first night shift, the first working day after induction day; he blew up his hands with a machine. It would disable him temporarily and required surgery and physiotherapy for a few months, until he was diagnosed with a carcinoma tumour.

After he had spent three months in chemo, my feet and hands were burning all the time. I was doing healing on him, with Reiki techniques, twenty-four/seven, with no breaks. He'd had one nuclear scan in between the diagnosis and the end of the chemo, as his oncologist said, "to see if the tumour would shrink as much as possible for better results in the surgery." When we went for the results of the second scan, the doctor could not hide his surprise at what he saw on his screen. He commented, "Such a good chemotherapy! Now we can increase the percentage to 50 per cent chance of survival.

In my heart, I knew we were being assisted in a miraculous way towards his cure.

We were already engaged with his medical condition, going to oncologists, laboratories, scanners, urologists, and chemo treatments for three consecutive months, followed by major surgery. It took six hours, and he was transferred to a nurse station for a few days, before being able to go to his room at the hospital. I was going twice a day to visit him on my own and once with my son, spending the weekends with him until he was able to leave the hospital and come back home. He had one crisis at the nurse station and was assisted through the emergency. My son and I never forgot that episode; we still remember all the nurses, doctors, and caregivers running around. It lasted probably a few minutes but seemed much longer for us. He survived and was discharged from the hospital completely clean.

We all saved his life together, and a new life would be born for each one of us, with a different perspective; a new life as a newborn, and everything would be very different from now on. My husband mumbled some words when he was still under the anaesthetics' effects that I will hear forever. I knew that he was suffering the worst lesson of his entire life, and I was there. I could not do more than I did, though I wished I could. I lost my man forever, and it would be the beginning of another painful journey. So again I found that writing about my feelings, I could feel better and healed.

Today in my heart space,
The serenity flows like a fog,
Cooling down the emotion, which
Used to move my body towards yours.
In our most sacred intimacy,
When we would fulfil our desires,
From the deepest of our souls fiercely
To the fresh and fragranced bed's sheets getting wet.
Today in my heart space remained the love,
Pure and flowing like a light breeze,
Fogging our wholeness in only one space;
Teaching us and replacing all that was hidden,
Making bigger and showing me,
My real and great feelings those used to be
Disguised by the fire of our passion!

Back home, I went out for full-time study in community service for twelve months, which still would be helping at home, with my son at school. Once the course was finished, I started working full time and became the main source of income for my family.

Everything seemed to be going fine, and I started a home-based business project. So I had family, a full-time job, and a home business to keep myself busy. It was all because I wanted to forget I was a human being. I sometimes laboured until five in the morning to make things work, with no regrets, until the day my husband was coming from one of his travels overseas. I asked him to get a check-up, participating in a national bowel-cancer campaign for those over fifty. In the beginning, he refused and I insisted, so he followed the instructions, and ten days later, his results were back.

In the first trial, one of five is positive to go to the next check, and he was the one. And once more, there we were. We still had the chance to not receive any bad news on the second check. Again, another one of five would be positive, and he was. At this time, it was like another bomb held with more patience, but not with less frustration and stress for him. He was always asking the question, "Why does this happen to me?"

I settled things at work for a few days off, put the business on hold, and we went back to his journey. Another biopsy test, and this time the luck was with us: there was no bad news, and the tumour was not malignant. However, there would be another major and difficult surgery to remove it, due to his primary surgery. It took another six hours, and the surgery was successful. It all started back up again, going between home, work, and hospital until discharge time, and then we were about to celebrate life again, relieved.

I saw my life in pieces. I was tired. I lost my man in my forties. I felt empty with no companion, no man, no love, and no perspective. All my spiritual lessons were good, but I suddenly started to feel that life could end at any time; I still had my job, which kept me alive. I was already receiving counselling alone; I had tried to do it with my husband, but he had given me his ultimatum: his way or the highway, as he wanted to go back to live in South America. That was something I had tried so many times, and it never worked for me. My son didn't want to go either, and he was only fifteen years old and my source of light and love. So I took the highway and left home.

I remember that my counsellor was worried about me and referred me to another professional, as she was leaving for Christmas holidays. The other doctor, after seeing me twice, found that we were progressing, but she said, "I need you do a test for me; an informal one. It's a book of self-help, and we find it very useful to assess your state of being. From that result, we will work out what will be the next step."

I asked her, "What would the possible steps be?"

She said, "If we find that you are going into a depressive state, I have to speak with you and refer you to your general practitioner."

I agreed with her; however, I had my own personal ways concerning medication. I would try any alternative treatment before starting taking tablets of any sort.

I purchased the book and went straight to that page to take the test.

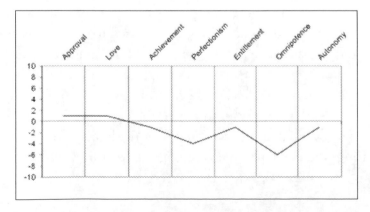

Once I completed the test and read through a few pages of that great book, *Feeling Good,* by David D. Burns, MD, I realized that I really needed to try something on my way. Simply working long hours would not be the solution for my problem. I was thinking and meditating about those results. It wasn't that I understood completely what it was all about technically; however, my knowledge about statistics and the meanings of the words themselves were convincing me that I needed to find the cause or causes for these test results. One thing I knew: my self-esteem was very low, and it had been for a very long time. It was hard for me to accept that time counted. I was assured that things had changed with my marriage status.

I remembered that I had read about a Buddhist teaching, something to the effect of when we are in our teenage years and someone or something insults us, we impulsively react at the moment with words or anger, and sometimes physically. When we are around our forties, we first think about it before responding to any attack; and when we are around our fifties, we go and meditate about it, as we know that if we are reacting to something, there is something inside us to be fixed. We do not take it further, to any response, but we appreciate and thank the source of it that is pointing us to our next lesson to be learned about ourselves and grow.

I had applied the teaching to that insulting test result, and I was open to move towards something that, for me, would be the light at the end of the tunnel. I have to confess that the idea of being treated by a psychotherapist was already overcoming a challenge. However, for me, it would have gone too far. I would have to find the way to turn that table around and start to move in a different direction!

I also had a group of people I would go to for self- and spiritual development, once a week. Jay and Jon are of teachers, extremely devoted to helping people on their path, and I believe they really make a difference in people's lives. She has many books published about her work, and they are amazing masters. I feel grateful that my path was drawn to their teachings at such an important and decisive time of my life. Every Tuesday for eleven weeks I was attending our meetings, which were vital for me and my learning. I used to travel forty-nine kilometres on the freeway south and another nine kilometres up the hills to get to their house, on a route where there was only you, trees, the moon, and kangaroos, with no cellular phone services at the beginning of the evening. At the end of the meetings, about ten thirty, we again had to go nine kilometres back to reach the freeway again, plus the forty-nine kilometres back home. That was all part of my therapy. Sometimes you could turn the lights off and still see the beauty of the moonlight bathing the eucalyptus surrounding the road in its ascending and descending curves and feel like you'd been taken to heaven.

Love still was my moving force and I still had it in my heart, stronger than ever. I was held by that love, and it took me up once a week to sit on God's lap and rest for a few hours, before coming back down the hill and starting to learn how to rescue myself from my misery.

I had my best friend there, waiting for me anytime I wanted to go, also in my spare time: the ocean. It would be my therapy room for the next seven months of my life.

I remembered Helen. She had tried her best for love, and she gave her life for her loving way to be. As she used to say: "I prefer to do things in a peaceful way." She had done everything she thought would be possible to sort things out with love. I am sure she is happy, no matter where she is. She was brave.

Chapter Seven

If you see yourself as one point inside your universe and it seems to be just a small point, remember it is your point, and that is what really matters at this point.
—Elvira Divina Fernandes

In Command of a Matchbox

We were sailing the Gulf of Carpentaria, back on the deck of *Task Fish,* after all the duties were carried out to start sailing.

We could always be surprised by different friends from that beautiful blue water.

Most days, depending on where we stopped, we would see turtles, dugongs, sharks, crocodiles, and dolphins. It was a shame we could not see even one single whale all along our journey, even though it was the season for them to travel to Australia's east, north, and northeast coasts. We had sailed around five thousand nautical miles on this journey, and unbelievably, there was no sign of one whale.

The wind was perfect, and we were only on our sails that morning. The vessel was gliding in a beautiful and harmonious way. I had spoken with my son the night before, and I said to him, "I am tired, son; I don't think I am going to make it to the end of this journey."

As usual, he was always encouraging me to go ahead. He said, "Mom, you came to this point, and now you think you are not going to make it? That doesn't sound like you!" He added, "Please don't worry about me. I am fine, and everything is under control. So you have no reason to interrupt your dream. I am sure you can accomplish it up to the end."

I had missed being with him on his eighteenth birthday, and that was painful. I really missed hugging him, catching up and being around him, but we also both knew that our separation was fundamental for both of us to find our own path in our lives.

His words of support counted very much, and it seemed we were aligned with Mother to Earth. That day, we didn't have one or two of them, but we had an entire pod of giant dolphins swimming under and around us for about half an hour. There were fourteen, and their playfulness was the most beautiful thing that could happen to me that morning. From the deck, I was playing with them like a kid, making sounds with my voice. They looked like they enjoyed that, so I filmed them, and that day's trip was even worthier.

I could feel the movement of my body dancing at my debut party, as well as the freshness of the waterfall when swimming with a boyfriend, friends, and siblings, splashing water on each other. I remembered enjoying life with the best feelings of my twenties, celebrations of new years on Brazilian beaches, nights and nights of Carnival with friends. All the good fun came up with that magical choreography under my feet, and nothing could work better for my soul, mind, and body than exactly that at this point in my life.

I imagined how far I could have gone if I had chosen to take antidepressant tablets and how much I would have missed doing that. As I mentioned before, we know more about our boundaries and conditions than any professional in any area of any health system. I am not saying that we don't have to go for professional advice when we don't feel healthy. But I would say that we have our own inner voice, which counts, and if we are not able to hear it, we also need to seek help in finding tools to improve it.

Our intuition is a great guidance for us. I learnt that we really will grow if we step out of our comfort zone and expose ourselves to different situations and circumstances. In doing so, we test our limits, and we know better about ourselves. So we expand our limits, and we create new comfort zones, living within them until we feel like we need another push. Lack of satisfaction should be considered motivation for improvement, not a reason to give up and fall. That can be our inner voice's first signal, and we know that. We can look back and see many instances when people we know found their biggest success and fulfilment just when they turned the corner.

We will probably still be feeling like I did when we were in the middle of the Gulf of Carpentaria. As I sailed while Will rested, I could look around and feel like I was in command of a matchbox; that was the yacht's size compared to the vastness of the ocean around me. Our lives in eternity and in the vastness of the universe reaches, have a point where we realise differences but never see a real limit. The only certainty we have to seek is that we are in command of who we really are, what we feel and choose.

A few days later, we went through another hard time, facing strong currents and winds. It is hard to explain; it was like we had to sail at a negative speed, due to the current. It takes time and persistence, patience and the ability to deal with a situation where you have no calm and enough water to stop and wait, with the wind blowing easterly and the current against you. You have to go in zigzags to advance one mile, when you should have gone five miles in the same period of time. This situation is very stressful and demanding, and we were just starting to turn around the first side of the "U" of the Gulf of Carpentaria. We hoped that when we turned around, we'd have more favourable winds and tides, conditions appropriate to sail and to anchor at the end of each day. That was the first time we were following this trajectory.

We didn't know very much, only the weather forecast and what the charts told us. Even having the latest edition of the charts on board, we had learned that in some places, their accuracy wasn't high. Underwater circumstances could have changed after the charts were printed and released; in some of those cases, we were left just with hope. But anytime I expected something bad, I was always looking forward to a positive outcome. Most importantly, I was always extremely faithful for the good!

We managed to sail up to a town called Weipa, where we would stay for a few days for supplies before heading to the bottom of the gulf. It would be around four hundred nautical miles and would probably take around ten days. The plan was to spend one month sailing inside the gulf, close to the shore. By our calculations, we could do it and reach Darwin at the beginning of October and be in Windham no later than the beginning of November.

We left Weipa. I was happy, as with a bit more experience I realised that I would be more comfortable after buying a foldable chair to have in the cockpit, for those times I wasn't able to stay inside the vessel. It would give me seasickness; outside on the deck, it would not be possible because of weather conditions: too sunny or sometimes strong winds with high swells. I would not have those long hours navigating while standing up in the cockpit. The winds still were not the best, but we had to leave, to follow the schedule. That was another huge challenge! There were no islands to offer protected anchorage; shallow water was all along the coast, which would make it hard to anchor the vessel. Strong easterly winds were against us, with strong currents and low tides not allowing us entry into the rivers' mouths. We stopped once in one river, where the tide was favourable to get into it, but not to get out of it in the early morning. We could not anchor at the beaches, as the winds were too strong and the tides too low. We had no choice after two days of waiting for better tides; we had to leave anyway, as it would get lower and lower. We tried and got bogged on the beach.

We waited until the water rose a bit, and at sunset, we took off against all odds and with not many options. For three days, we were sailing all day and, up to ten in the evening, making twenty nautical miles per day. The vessel bounced against the four-metre swell, sailing back and forwards to get proper stops for the night. When we could not cope with that any longer, we stopped, figuring anything would be less dangerous than keeping up with those circumstances.

We were sixty miles outside of Weipa when we decided to change course. The proposition was: if I did not want to go across the gulf, as we had arranged at the beginning of the journey, I would be brought back to Weipa, sailing with the winds behind us, which would be easy. From there, I would take a plane back home, and Will would find someone in town to continue on the journey with him. We would not keep to the original course, to try different and better solutions. Facing that challenge, I thought nothing could be worse than that. I said to myself, *I am confident in what I have learnt up to this point, and I trust myself. I trust again in my instincts, and with my faith in the good, I will make it. This vessel is reliable, more than Will's first vessel, which didn't give him a safe and pleasant journey five years previous, doing the same journey. With the wind coming from behind us, or with no wind, one way or another, we will be better than this life-threatening situation we are in now.*

I said to the captain, "Okay, I will go across with you. When and from where? What are we going to do now?"

It was around nine at night, and we had completed eighteen hours of sailing to make less than twenty nautical miles. We had nowhere to stop and anchor, unless we turned around and sailed back until we got a bit more water under us. At the closest possible point to the shore, we could sleep a bit, when the wind would allow us. So we started to sail back, and after about ten nautical miles, we stopped and had some rest.

In the morning, we had a wind of just five knots, and the weather was calling for another high coming close to us in the next three days. It would give us three nights and four days to be protected from the next high-pressure air mass at the other side of the gulf, if we could manage to keep an average speed of 4.5 knots along the crossing, above sixty metres' depth of water. It would mean sailing around four hundred nautical miles up to the west side of the gulf in two nights and three days, with no stopping.

We all planned and agreed that if there was no wind, we should turn the engine on, to keep up the average speed, so we would proceed as planned. Starting in the morning, we would pull out the spinnaker sail, as it was appropriate and suitable for the gentle wind. We were expecting the wind to increase, so we would make the changes with the sails, and off we went.

Now it was time to create a new work plan, as we had to split between us two the times to take over and sail while the other would sleep.

I was sailing from seven in the evening until one in the morning and then back again around four in the morning until ten or eleven. I was just having my meals and water, cordials, coffee and tea, navigating through equipment on the evening shifts and seeing the sunrises amaze me. I have no words to describe awakening with the ocean, without seeing anything around other than water.

After one day of navigating, Will brought the news that we would use the engine as little as possible, as he hadn't replaced the spent engine oil in Weipa, and we had only around one litre. It would be kept in case we had an emergency. The wind was falling, and with it our average speed. We had completed less than a third of the crossing. It was my night shift, and my speed was 1.8 knots. This was my reality: I was on the open water, in a vessel with no engine oil, sailing at that speed. Under the vessel I had sixty-five metres of depth; I could not see anything out there, other than the stars up in the sky. All was pitch black surrounding us. The captain was exhausted, and had fallen into a deep sleep, the yacht was just drifting, and nothing could be done except keep an eye on the equipment. It was on automatic pilot, so there was not much to look at, just to be aware! But what could I also be aware of? Suddenly I realized that we were not accomplishing the planned average speed, and it meant we'd be vulnerable to the wind coming with the next high. God knows if we would miss Australia and end up in Papua New Guinea or East Timor. Who knows?

I felt nothing could scare me, any changes on my heart.

I remembered that I was told by a fortune teller that I would never be in the open water without falling into panic for just been there. That was the opposite. That unknown situation was now known, and that was not bad to me. The unexpected bad part hadn't happened. I was there, drifting, just waiting for the wind to blow. I felt like if the high could come, blow me out of Australian's water, I would only have to adjust the sails, simply that. I just had peace in my heart. I was just feeling in between the stars and the waters. I again felt a sensation of being seated on God's lap, being in heaven, and just enjoying the feeling of being whole.

After three nights—one more than planned—plus the following twelve hours, we arrived the other side at Bremer Island, Australian land. I had been aligning myself with my source and sending that love and peace from my heart to my loved ones, including to one of my brothers, who fell ill while I was in the middle of my journey. The wind was still calm and blowing us kindly. There was a perfect harmony between my wishes, and Mother Nature was swaying with me, conducting me in its supreme love and rhythm.

On August 30, we left Bremer Island, headed towards English Company Island. It started to feel like heaven again for a few more days. The land in the Northern Territory and its islands is magnificent and had compensated for all the hassle from bad weather and natural inconveniences facing us all along the way.

Chapter Eight

*Surround your needs to the universe. Keep your faith, trust,
and hopes up, and you will be amazedly surprised.*
—Elvira Divina Fernandes

The Freshwater Miracle

I have heard that God doesn't place the solution for our problems in our pocket, but it will be there when we need it, if we have faith. I know now that in some way, we need to have a reason to push us to meet the desire to dive into a new adventure, to get distracted and not let negativity to overtake us.

Hard work was part of our daily life, demanding physical strength. It was a challenge demanding courage, and more than anything else, there was incredible faith coming from inside me, saying that I have the right to have rights in life, and to use life and honour it. Live it intensively and experience it. For the first time, I was feeling that I could live without fear. It reminds me of when I used to live in Brazil and I learnt that if you trip over something when you are walking, you just think: *God is with me, and nothing will put me down.* We learn a lot during our lives, tips and advice, but for some reason, we discard some of them, and some of them we intend to practice, and it works impressively.

We were looking for fresh water since we left Weipa, our last supply stop. Along the journey, we managed to use the available freshwater very well. It was routine to have a salty bath every day, and sometimes, when we were close to abundant fresh water, a good splash with it. Otherwise, Will would not mind. But I used to rinse with a fast shower at abundant times, and when the water was short, I used to just wipe my body with freshwater and have less salt on me.

The cleaning and dishes were done with salt water, and we had spring water for beverages and very limited cooking. We had our daily menu—some vegetables, kept frozen, some tinned food for salads. The main meals were fresh fish, oysters, and crabs. If we anchored in a river's mouth, we had crabs or fish or both; if we anchored close to beaches and rocks, we had oysters or fish or both, and if we anchored at an island with reefs, we had reef fish.

We also had fresh coconuts and wild almonds to enjoy from the wilderness.

As I said before, the daily work was very demanding and hard, even enjoyable tasks like fishing, crabbing, and collecting oysters from the rocks. To catch a fish in that area demands energy in fighting with sharks constantly getting hooked before you can beat them and pull in your catch, as well pulling the dinghy's anchor in and out. With the crabs came other hard work: catching or setting up bait, throwing pots on the high tides, checking them after each hour, and pulling in all the heavy gear and cleaning up.

With the oysters came bending backs and knees, racing with the tides, walking on the slippery rocks, and watching for crocs. But it is no sacrifice for those whose love it. The most incredible feeling is in the interaction with the ocean, the most remote and isolated places, the forests, animals, birds, and our integration and living with the light of the sunsets and sunrises directed at you. Sleeping and sometimes awakening to the full moon's light on your face through the hatch.

We were seeking freshwater with no joy after more than two months from Weipa. We were already six months into the journey, and I was missing my son dearly.

There was no way to know how much water we had in the fresh-water tank. We had only eleven litres of spring water to drink, with thirty days still ahead before arriving in Darwin. It had been a long while with no more fresh-water showers, neither long nor fast ones. We could only perform a very slight wiping-off after a salty bath. The charts had no indication of freshwater on our next islands. There were several small islands, and we kept stopping every day, anchoring at a different one with the intent of finding any source of freshwater, even if it was for bathing, but nothing was happening.

We just knew that the fresh-water tank wasn't even at half, so we might have to drink that water after finishing the eleven litres of spring water left.

Like any other day, we set up the sails, taking off for the next island, and I went to the deck. That morning, I felt that I was close to the end, and the journey still had tough times ahead. I wished badly that it would end in some way. I could not ask for more than I had. I had so much anyway: lessons, beautiful food, adventure, peace, growth, work, exciting life experience, so I wasn't missing anything from that journey.

I tried to frame a miracle and imagine myself going back to my son, my family overseas, and visiting my brother. I pondered what would be the best for me at this point. I really didn't realise what was happening there. In the deepest part of my heart, I just wanted freshwater.

We sailed all morning and planned to anchor at Wessel's Island. I confess I was done!

I felt myself drawn and melting with the ocean's water, in my mind, in my heart, in my being, as it was not worthwhile to worry any longer. I recalled a thought from the Master Dalai Lama: "When you cannot see any way out, why do you fall in stress and worry about the situation?"

I assumed my weakness and threw myself on the deck, trying to get some sleep or at least forget about everything.

I wasn't even eating lunch properly that day, which had never happened before. But I carried on with my duties and had the job done until I was called to wind in the sails to anchor. It was about two in the afternoon. There was a beautiful and isolated bay at the island, and we could see the bottom through the clear water.

We could see something different on the white-sand beach from far away. It looked different from all the others. After we anchored, we dropped the dinghy down as usual to scout around. The tide was going out, and we started to walk towards the beach. My eyes widened, and my heart started pumping with the most incredible joy. I jumped out and ran towards it; there, three metres from the tide line in the middle of the white sand were a few red rocks and a source of the most delicious freshwater I have ever tasted in my life! I started to clear around and dig a small pool, surrounding it with a few rocks and sand. It was crystalline, and it was definitely the best bath on my tanned, salty, and dried body.

I felt like the most beautiful, happiest, and luckiest person on Earth. I had a little ritual with my salty-water bath, freshwater, and the silence of that magnificent place. I dropped my mind and my body and only enjoyed the magical miracle gratefully.

The following morning, I went back to the shore very early with buckets, gallons, and all my laundry. It was like a party day, and it deserved to start with the sunrise. Will decided to go to walk around and explore, and I laid things down and started my meditation. I threw my rug on the sand and lay down beside my latest found treasure. I dared not miss even its sounds, running smoothly over those little rocks and filing my little pond. I started with long, deep breaths, closed my eyes, and went off that world for about an hour, as usual. That place was a beautiful sanctuary where we can dispose of our physical bodies for a while and let our soul play its role in whatever the moment is.

I finished my relaxing meditation and started to come back to that great physical spot. I was called to look at the ocean, and less than ten metres away, I saw a crocodile just standing still and looking at me. He was as curious about me as I was about him. My movement immediately made him swim away slowly and hide behind a big rock. I started to film him as he swung around; as soon as I would stop, he would stop too and swim back and forwards. We stayed playing hide-and-seek for a few hours that morning until he decided to give up and leave. He was a six-foot-long young croc, not like those harmful giants. He was just a baby, and it was my very lucky and beautiful day to enjoy with my freshwater and the supply. I ended my trip abundantly, with as much freshwater as I could. We spent about two more weeks at Wessel's Islands and the English Group Islands before finally heading to Darwin.

Will's mother and her sister turned up for three days, sailing close to Darwin. We had a good time, enjoying two days in the water and the rest of the week in a marina before we sailed up to the end of our journey another week later, anchoring in the Gulf of Cambridge, north of Western Australia State.

My sailing journey was finished. I had put all of me into that journey, and I have no regrets. I did it all with my heart. Each day, I worked and tried to figure out about the potential relationship with Will and still remained open to give ourselves a go to make things work. I had learnt that we are fortunate, not for a big bank account and assets, but we are fortunate when we focus on the positive side of things and people. So I closed my eyes to the negative points of our relationship, as there were many positive points. Even then, I could not have time or opportunity to think too much. I was dearly missing my son, and I had a few personal things to sort about my life. The pressure was unbearable, not having the freedom to choose. I flew back to Perth, and I wish I had a chance to try, as I said; however, I haven't. But I know that my free spirit would not allow me to live isolated from the rest of the world, as the relationship's purpose was from Will. There were conditions I would never be able to cope with, so I made sure things stopped before it got worse. He sent my personal belongings back, and I cancelled my booked flight back up north and decided to get back close to my son and to myself. Once more, I felt much stressed, as I was back on land. I missed being on the ocean twenty-four/seven.

Those old habits were making me wear my bikinis and go to my backyard, seeking the water. It took me months to settle down. The negotiations with Will also took my balance away, and I went to see my doctor once more. She immediately prescribed me antidepressants again. As I'd never had any of those tablets, I went to the pharmacist for more details. She explained me what it was about. But this time, I was stronger than before, so I could turn things back on track again. I also needed to go to Brazil to see my brother and my family, to give a little hand to my son with his journey moving around.

I found my son more mature, and we were both undergoing a big transformation. We still had a lot to deal with until things got better with our family. We had housing to sort out for both of us, as the circumstances still were not appropriate. I knew I should leave soon, as my brother's situation became severe. I needed to go and see him, be with him, my lovely sister-in-law and kids, as well as all my siblings and mother. It had been more than three years since I'd seen them all. We were always very family-oriented, and that brother was the first to become severely ill. That idea was making me sad, the thought that I might not see him alive again. My son once again stood up for himself as one brave man, at eighteen, supporting me and taking his own journey again.

I also always found that if we can keep ourselves busy taking care of others a bit more, helping them with their needs, we forget our frustrations and live more happily. For me, it was my alternative medicine, to avoid taking tablets and find work to do. Being paid helps with your living; not being paid, if you can, helps others living and keeping busy, mind and heart.

And in my spare time, the ocean is there for me. If there is no ocean, we will find a park, a bush, a backyard. Even if you are not able to access nature's aspects physically, just throw yourself in a chair, bed, or mat on the floor of your house, and go off in your memories, where you were in contact with nature. Reconnect, and let a bridge be built between you and your consciousness, surrounding yourself with the peace and strength you need to move to the next step. Try harder, before you feel you're falling again.

Once more, I think that David D. Burns is right in his *Feeling Good* book. Once you can win for the first time over your depressive state by yourself, if you have to face it again, it will be easier to defeat. That was the case for me. I opened the gate to my inner strength, and that was a personal meeting with God. That was my personal way to grow and balance my energies positively. I had proof that what is good for me never comes effortlessly.

Chapter Nine

I am a unique creature of nature. I am rare, and there is value in all rarity; therefore, I am valuable. I am the end of a product of thousands of years of evolution; therefore, I am better equipped in both mind and body than all the emperors and wise men who preceded me. But my skills, my mind, my heart, and my body will stagnate, rot and die lest I put them to good use. I have unlimited potential. Only a small portion of my brain do I employ; only a paltry amount of my muscles do I flex. A hundredfold or more can I increase my accomplishments of yesterday and this I will do, beginning today?
—Og Mandino

I Asked and I Had It!

The winter was almost over. For a tropical area on our planet, a breeze touching us reminds us that the page is supposed to be turned, and we have to keep moving forward.

Photo by A. Wilson

Many times on my sailing journey, I looked around me and could only see the vast magnificence of wildlife, waters, beaches, forests, islands, mountains. I wished with the deepest part of my heart that I would be with my family soon. Being so integrated into that natural environment made me feel peaceful, complete, and content, so I asked to go back, and once more, there I was.

Before I left Australia, we had turmoil. Once more, I ended up seeing a doctor, and the situation seemed really bad to her, so she prescribed me some tablets. I left her office and went to the pharmacy. The pharmacist asked me if I ever had that medication before, and I said no. Then she offered to print out the medication's information, and I agreed, thanked her, paid for it, and left. As usual, there were side effects similar to the symptoms. That's what I was told, and it doesn't make sense to me. Anyway, I tried them, and I was told the tablets would start to help me in one week. However, the side effects were worse than the stress, and they overtook me after the first tablet, making my body itch with a terrible skin rash, so I had to stop.

My son and I were homeless, and we had to find a place to live in the middle of a housing crisis in the entire metropolitan area of Perth. I was back to work, and the time was running fast. I engaged myself in new studies, booked another of those great and joyful workshops. There was one thing I needed to bring into my life again, before any tablet or doctor's visit: more from the ocean. I was missing it badly—to be in the water, swimming, fishing, sailing, or at least a bit more than only going for a swim after work. It was great therapy for me. I looked up to the sky and yelled with my heart in my mind: *Universe, please send me someone to help me with that. I need to go back to the water. I need company, and I need a spiritual being. I don't want any anger in my life. I want someone just spiritual.*

One week later, I met my spiritual companion at the beach, and he said to me, "Would you like to teach me about meditation? I can teach you to dive."

I thought that my last journey would be my highest challenge at fifty-two, but I had no idea that I was able to became a scuba diver two years later and start a new journey twenty metres underwater and meditate there, connecting with my ancestors, with my source. I so love the ocean and its vastness; going deeper for me was to feel hugged by Mother Earth's energy, connecting with it to the point of feeling able to be in heaven here and now, in the exact way we choose to be.

Throughout this book, I have shared more about my spiritual life than my sexual life experiences, as I am more a spiritual person than anything else. I cannot neglect what has, besides my spirituality, guided me to where I am today. It was my own boldness, exploration, and decision to embrace my sexuality with the same care and respect for myself and others, as well as honouring what we call "God."

I have discovered on my life's journey that sexuality is the most powerful and physical tool used to bring our physical human body closer to our highest good. This, in one way or another, has been taken from us ever since we stepped onto the planet. We arrived here with a physical body supporting the great weight of our spirit and soul and encompassing many needs. We were not asked by God to cast aside or judge anything as good or bad. Instead, we were granted the free will to enjoy our own power and knowledge whilst walking on Earth.

Regardless of what we have been taught, every living being has been granted its own inner light and purity. Each living being embodies compassion, unconditional love, freedom, understanding, forgiveness, and is born free of judgement. God provides a common, free path for all living beings to walk on. We do, as human beings, make the choice either to project our light to help ourselves and others or to keep our light shining within. God is light and is encapsulated within every being unconditionally. Our physical body is our tool and our gift. Our physical body enables us to carry God within to protect, guide, and help us to enlighten and influence the planet peacefully.

We will always have time to contemplate our choices and to trust in our inner guidance. We can always protect and nurture our inner light, spirituality, and sexuality to fulfil our journey towards complete wholeness of body, soul, heart, and mind.

Books references

1. The Power of Now – Eckart Tole
2. The New Earth- Eckart Tole
3. The Power of Intention, Dr. Wayne W. Dyer
4. The Power of Attraction, Dr. Wayne W. Dyer
5. Excuse Begone, Dr. Wayne D. Dyer
6. You can heal yourself, Louise Hay
7. Opening to Channel, Sanya and Duane Paker
8. Hands That Heal, Echo Bodine
9. Archangels & Ascended Masters, Doreen Virtue
10. Angel Medicine, Doreen Virtue
11. Angel Therapy, Doreen Virtue
12. Angel Visions, Doreen Virtue
13. Words of Wisdom, and The Art of happiness, Dalay Lama
14. A tea Spoon of Courage, Bradley Trevor Greive
15. Ego, attachment and Liberation, Lama Yesle
16. Facing Cancer and Searching for solution, Liz Byrski
17. The Art of War, Sun Tzu
18. Zen tarot, Osho
19. Spiritual Science of the Stars, Pete Stewart
20. Feeling Good, The New Mood Therapy, David D. Burns
21. The God Light Volume II, Jackie Lindsay
22. Don't think as a human, book I Lee Carroll, from the series of Kryon
23. Lifting the Veil, (The new energy Apocalipse, Lee Carroll, Kryon Book Eleven
24. The Twelve Layers of DNA, (An Esoteric Study of the Mastery within)
25. The Big Book of Angels Angelic Encounters, Expert Answers Listening and working with your guardian angel, by the editors of beliefnet
26. Angels, Gods and goddesses, Oracle Cards and Guide Book, Toni Carmine Salermo
27. Healing Energies, Understanding and using hands-on-healing – Bruce Way
28. The Prophet, kahlil Gibran
29. The Trilogy, Og Mandino.

October 26, 2017

Dear Customer:

Thank you for your purchase of *Evolutionary Multi-Objective System Design: Theory and Applications*, by Nadia Nedjah, Luiza De Macedo Mourelle, and Heitor Silverio Lopes.

On page xi, in the Table of Contents, Mouloud Koudil is incorrectly listed as a contributor to Chapter 9,

On page 171, the first page of Chapter 9, Mouloud Koudil is incorrectly listed as a chapter contributor.

We sincerely regret any inconvenience this may have caused you. Please
let us know if we can be of any assistance regarding this title or any other titles that Taylor & Francis publishes.

Best regards,
Taylor & Francis
978-1-4987-8028-5